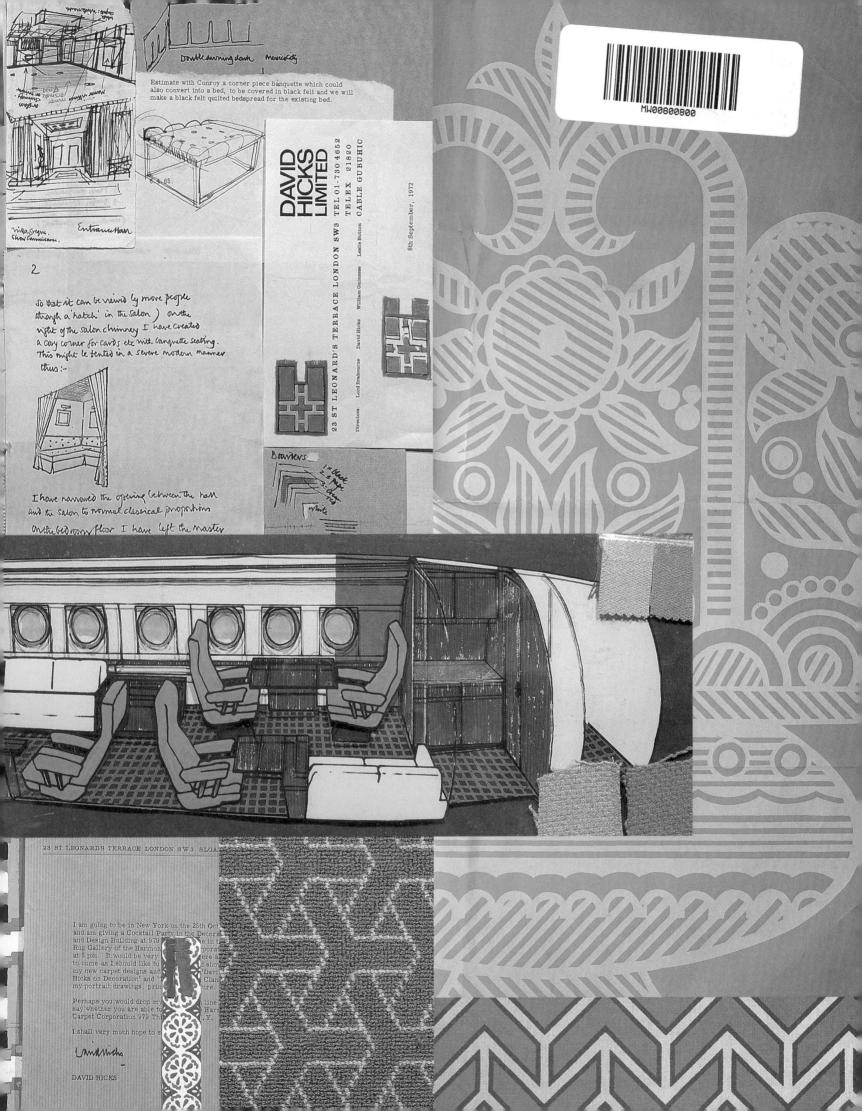

DAVID HICKS: DESIGNER

DAVID HICKS: DESIGNER

ASHLEY HICKS

SCRIPTUM EDITIONS

For Allegra, the second great designer in my life.

First published by Scriptum Editions
565 Fulham Road, London SW6 1ES

Created by Co & Bear Productions (UK) Ltd.
Copyright © 2003 Co & Bear Productions (UK) Ltd & The Estate of David Hicks.
Text © Ashley Hicks (2003)
Foreword © Tom Ford (2003)
Photographs © The Estate of David Hicks (2003), (unless otherwise stated see p.216)

Publishers Beatrice Vincenzini & Francesco Venturi
Design Pritty Ramjee, Karen Watts & Ashley Hicks
Editor Nikky Twymann
Publishing Assistant Ruth Deary

Printed and bound in Italy,
at Officine Grafiche De Agostini.

First edition
10 9 8 7 6 5 4 3 2 1

ISBN 1 902686 19 5

BOOKS BY DAVID HICKS:

David Hicks on Decoration 1966
David Hicks on Living – with Taste 1968
David Hicks on Bathrooms 1970
David Hicks on Decoration – with Fabrics 1971
David Hicks on Decoration – 5 1972
The David Hicks Book of Flower Arranging 1976
Living with Design 1979
Garden Design 1982
Style and Design 1987
Cotswold Gardens 1995
My Kind of Garden (ed Ashley Hicks) 1999

ALSO BY ASHLEY HICKS:

Ashley & Allegra Hicks: Design Alchemy 2002

THE WORDS

THE PICTURES

Foreword

When I first became aware of interior design and decorative arts, in the late 1960s and 1970s, David Hicks was enjoying his heyday as a society decorator. His style was inimitable. With his signature lacquered walls and cinematic uplighting, Hicks brought a very modern sense of drama and sophistication to the houses of his clients. He pioneered an eclectic mixture of old with new, placing reupholstered Louis XVI chairs alongside Lucite tables, or planting Knoll tulip chairs in stately salons.

Hicks was very much a decorator, which is not exactly the same thing as an interior designer. The designer devises efficient solutions to questions of space; decorators impose their own personal, often idiosyncratic vision to that space, using trademark techniques. Hicks had an Englishman's fearless relationship to colour and he knew how to use it. In his hands, scarlet, pink or orange became handsome and civilised, never flamboyant. And he flouted convention with spectacular use of pattern on pattern, declaring that it gave a room 'guts and distinction'.

Everything Hicks did, he did with conviction. His clients, as well as the thousands of people who bought his successful series of decorating books, followed his dictates to the letter. For a certain kind of rich, modern clientele — wealthy 30-year-olds leading cosmopolitan lifestyles — a David Hicks interior was the height of chic. A little bold, a little eccentric and quite luxurious, he created a slick, Park Avenue version of the 1960s and 1970s.

His palette may have been wild, but the end result was inevitably tailored and restrained. He excelled in creating luxe interiors with a distinctly masculine feel. Like a great storyteller or art director setting a scene, Hicks added atmosphere and character to a room through fastidious attention to detail. Fanatical about tablescapes, he felt that the arrangement of pictures, flowers and objects on a side-table was as crucial to a room's ambience as the furniture or artwork on the walls.

Refusing to follow old protocols, Hicks would gloss the walls of a country house's game room in deep aubergine, put a mod Joe Colombo chair against historic, Edwardian columns, and paint the ping-pong table red. He translated the radical design of the era into a language he knew his well-heeled clients could understand. Testament to his vision, the rooms still look elegant and sophisticated to this day.

Hicks himself was well-travelled and well-versed in the history of design and decor. He always said his greatest source of inspiration was the past. His talent was the unique way in which he propelled those ideas into the future, working with what already existed – mouldings, antiques and overstuffed sofas – and charging them with the more modern energy of Corbusier chairs and contemporary art. Though he was a fixture on a some-what jet-set scene, moving between projects in Nassau and New York, Zurich and London, there was always a charming thriftiness to his approach. Antiques would be rescued from redundancy with bright, Pop-influenced upholstery or a coat of glossy paint; or a room would get a revamp, with yards of crimson silk draped around the windows.

'Decorating is the art of accentuating the best and covering up the worst,' Hicks once said. As a decorator, he was creating the setting for a certain kind of lifestyle, one where etiquette, chic and gracious entertaining were prized above all else.

If Hicks's work looks familiar today, it's because so many of the tricks that designers rely upon now owe a debt to him. Though much of his decor is iconic of the era, there is a strong, graphic quality that still holds up, thirty years later. It's a little ironic that the techniques which seemed so daring then – the slick, dark walls and graphic, patterned floors – have now been absorbed into design orthodoxy. In fact, Hicks's work has become something of a rulebook for instant elegance. I fall back on his tricks myself: if I need to make a room glamorous, I lacquer the walls in a dark colour.

Hicks derived pleasure from changing the surface of things, and perhaps that is what makes his work so appealing now. Today, we are quick to knock walls down and tear spaces apart, frequently ending up with environments that say more about the architect than the people who live there. Hicks made rooms to be lived in. He created homes that were rich with character, comfort and luxury. As people tire of minimalism, and as our fascination with cool, mid-century modernism fades, the time seems right to celebrate Hicks's unique vision and enduring legacy.

Tom Ford, LONDON, 1ST JUNE 2002

A Window into Another World

My father was a great showman and loved nothing better than to lecture at some length about his achievements and creations, past and present. He would do this during *tête-à-tête* lunches in New York, during tea with our family in Oxfordshire or, more formally, to groups ranging from the tiny, like the Eton College Art Society or the Ewelme Women's Institute, to large audiences at the Royal Society of Arts in London or the Design Association of Atlanta. These more formal lectures were accompanied by slides, and invariably began with the same image – a grainy picture of an old magazine cover which he said had been his first inspiration to become a decorator.

He was in the army, aged 17 (and doing the obligatory National Service) when he bought the first issue of *House & Garden* published after the War. It had, he said, 'a brilliant yellow cover with "House & Garden" in very elegant black type'. He described it as 'very organized, very formal. I thought it was the most exciting thing I'd ever seen, absolutely wonderful. I devoured it, cover to cover. I read the words "interior decoration", which I'd never heard of before.'

My father described to me how he had longingly examined the magazine in the hideous surroundings of a small teashop near Chatham barracks. The café, its windows fogged up with breath and steam in the grim English winter, stank of rancid cooking oil and the sweaty soldiers who crowded its little tables. The beautiful magazine was like a window into another world, a world of elegance and sophistication.

He often described these early glimpses as 'another world' or 'pure magic', and indeed there is no small element of fantasy in the story of my father's life. As a child in an Essex village, Coggeshall, he would organize imaginary tea parties, to which he would invite, among others, Queen Victoria. His mother was always delighted to have such eminent guests in the house and would elaborately welcome 'Her Majesty' without the slightest indication that she doubted little David's insistence that the Queen had arrived, was now removing her coat and hat, needed more biscuits or another slice of cake, and so on. Certainly she never mentioned the inconvenient fact that the Queen had died thirty-five years before.

In his early years, fantasy was a form of escape from his mediocre surroundings, busily encouraged by a doting mother whose theatrical leanings had been frustrated by the strictures of middle-class life. Later on, when he succeeded in weaving elements of this fantasy into the reality of his own life, it gradually became obsessive. At the end, much of his time was spent arranging and rearranging the scenery and props in the private theatre of his world, that grand production he wrote and directed, and in which he starred.

May 1997

Less than a year before my father's death (he died on 29 March 1998), I made him sit down and talk to me about his early life and the start of his career. We had a vague idea of my writing his biography, which came to nothing, but it did prompt me to tape-record some of his memories. He had often wanted to have his biography written, and a journalist had started on one thirty years earlier, with its subject a precocious 38 years old. That had gone nowhere, as had numerous attempts since then, both biographical and autobiographical. Only 68, but looking much older, already very sick and perhaps feeling the end was not far off, he once again longed to see his life in print.

We sat in his garden at The Grove, his Oxfordshire home since 1980, in that sunny May weather that seems such a miracle in England. Some days we sat outside the drawing-room window, looking out at the sharply clipped *allées* of hornbeam and the far vista of his new chestnut avenue stretching to the horizon beyond the gates; on others, we sat in the Lime Room that he had created two years before, with walls of soft lime leaves and a quietly dripping fountain made from an old stone jar set up on a brick base. We sat there in two chairs of his own design. These are still there today, and often remind me of that absurdly formal little tableau – a father passing on his memories to his son.

I was helped by my father's passion for talking about himself, a subject that never ceased to fascinate him, and by his old man's clear memories of childhood. At times I could feel him wandering back sixty years, through the rooms of his childhood homes, through the elaborate halls of his memory. The details he recalled were incredibly vivid – descriptions of specific smells and colours; of bomb-ravaged London; of the aromatic lavender in Provence; of the deep-red blinds of his father's house, the sun beating down on them as they were pulled down by the housemaids, respectfully acknowledging a funeral passing by on the village street outside.

I was keen, above all, to get an insight into what had formed his style, his inimitable but much-imitated style, which I had always taken for granted (having grown up surrounded by it). Where did this come from, this curious obsession with dramatic interiors, with perfect objects arranged in perfect compositions; this tense and precise way of living that placed aesthetics above any other consideration? What were his earliest memories of glamour, of style, of what he invariably called 'good taste'? When had he first started to live in that way? Before turning to his early years and influences, I might say something of my own memories of my father, of growing up with him.

Private D. N. Hicks, off to basic training, 1946.

Altar Boy at the Temple to Taste

Looking back at the work in this book, I was first struck by how well I knew so much of it. Growing up with my father was very involving. As his only son, I was expected to follow his work very closely and I spent hours at every age poring over his elaborately assembled scrapbooks of press cuttings and photographs, which by the end numbered twenty-five volumes. Beautifully bound in black with scarlet leather labels stamped with his 'H' logo, his name and the book's date, these were always ranged in his country library, where they held an important, symbolic place as the sum of his life's achievements.

When I was a child, my father was one of my two great heroes. The other was my spectacular grandfather Lord Mountbatten, whose achievements – among which he was the last Viceroy of India in 1947 – were catalogued in even more tangible fashion than my father's, at Broadlands, his home in Hampshire. In this large and beautiful country house, my sisters (Edwina and India) and I, along with our Knatchbull cousins, would spend every Christmas as children, nursed in the myths and legends of my grandfather's family history, and those of his own life. There I would linger for hours by his sword table, where all of his ceremonial swords were laid out on black velvet, or in his uniform wardrobe, where his valet would patiently explain to me the precise use of each of his splendid military outfits.

A young boy is most easily seduced by things military, but visits to Broadlands came only once or twice a year, while Britwell (our own home in Oxfordshire) was a vivid and ever-changing temple to taste, a cathedral of David

House & Garden: 'a window into another world'.

The Gothic door to The Grove's garden, 1997, with clipped hornbeams beyond.

*The library at Britwell, 1978.
The scrapbooks, black and red,
are on the lower right.*

*Broadlands, Hampshire, the
garden front by 'Capability'
Brown.*

*Britwell Salome, Oxfordshire,
the garden front, with the
1760 chapel on the far right.*

Hicks style in which I played the part of junior altar boy. Many an afternoon of my childhood found me idling around one or other of the many photographers who were an almost-constant presence in the house, as it was photographed again and again for magazines all over the world. In the absence of uniforms and swords, a camera is a boy's best friend, especially a professional's large-format model on a towering tripod. I must have driven them insane with all my questions, but I was fascinated.

Being dispatched to boarding school aged 8 intensified my hero-worship, just as it did for all of us, closeted in our strange world of British male childhood. Fathers were hugely important and much-vaunted. While my grandfather's dwindling fame was exciting (our greatest collective interest was World War II and, so far as I had been given to understand, he had won the War single-handed), my father's fame was growing. In his frequent letters he would send me press cuttings, sketches, or mad diagrams illustrating the growth of his design 'empire'. The latter often depicted trees rooted in the 'rich Essex soil' of his childhood, with all his varied activities and products hanging from the branches, and me represented by an architect's set square sporting my initials.

Letters have so much importance at boarding school. While my mother wrote comforting updates on life at Britwell, news of family, my sisters and dogs – always the same length and in the same hand, and on the same immaculate paper – my father instead sent me exotic postcards from Los Angeles or Tokyo, letters on gossamer-thin Concorde paper complaining about the service on the new supersonic jet; letters in elaborate, stiff envelopes pinched from royal palaces, the crests on the back so embarrassingly large that I would turn bright red as the housemaster handed them to me. Often these huge envelopes opened to reveal a tiny memo page with 'love from Daddy' and nothing more. Others would contain long, complicated letters written several hours (and many gin and tonics) into a long-haul flight.

Letters from a Father

In January 1974, I was 10 years old. About to leave Britwell for America, my father wrote to me, 'the workmen are getting on fast in the wing and you will see a lot of changes when you come here on February 3rd. Ask them to unlock the passage so that you can go along and inspect.' Then, in November: 'Yesterday, with a horrid cold, I flew to Copenhagen to look for a suitable shop for Denmark. Tomorrow I fly to Belfast and drive out to the Duke of Abercorn's house which I am to redesign for father and son, wife and daughter-in-law to share – it's big enough – they've got 3 libraries. Dukes do tend to! On Wednesday the Shah of Persia's architect invited me to submit designs for the new palace on the Caspian Sea which is exciting…'

In March 1975, 'on the ground at Amsterdam en route to Bangkok via Teheran', he told me that he found it 'funny to think I'll have a shop here in 28 days and probably in Teheran too in a year…' Neither happened. In April, he wrote: 'I am en route for Geneva where I will see the B's flat which I saw once before, completely empty and hideous and now, a year later, I shall see it completely finished and lived in. Decoration by David Hicks by remote control, courtesy of Madame Vulliod.' (Fleur Vulliod was his Swiss associate for many years.) 'Tonight I stay with the Vulliods who are giving a dinner party for me. I always tell them that after flying and working I want a quiet evening with them alone but they always give a party! Luckily, however, she obeys implicitly all my other instructions.'

Again in April, 'the Aeroflot opening went well, in spite of 50 demonstrators, 80 police and 30 KGB men. The Civil Aviation Minister, who "aerofloted in" from Moscow, said he was very pleased with our work', on the interior of the Soviet Russian state airline's London offices on

Piccadilly. That November, 'on my way to Johannesburg in very bumpy weather...I'm reading the first two chapters of my new book... You can imagine the excitement in Johannesburg as André and Monique [his associates there] put the finishing touches to the shop prior to the "maestro" arriving tomorrow morning! They have press photographers coming out to the airport, wireless interviews, a lecture and magazine editors all laid on!'

The following January, he had been 'to Paris for two days and worked for M and Mme Schlumberger and for the University of Paris. I go to Windsor Castle to see the Queen about the Garter Room carpet and then on Feb 23 I leave for Arizona & Australia and Japan, Tokyo etc.' In March, he was 'Between Fiji and Sydney... I had a super day in S. Francisco, lunch in a fabulous restaurant which calmed my nerves, as on the way up from Palm Springs the jet was hit by "static discharge" which in plain English is lightning! It will be fun to stay in James Fairfax's guest room in Sydney as I designed it when I was there 4 years ago but have never seen it completed.'

For a young English boy stuck in a succession of provincial boarding schools, these letters were a window on to a wider world of glamour and excitement. My father's enthusiasm and sense of adventure were infectious, and everyone around him was captivated – not least his own son. I believed in him totally, and was fiercely proud of every achievement, every press cutting, every new shop, carpet design or book. I would beaver away at my own 'design work', chiefly military to start with, whole mechanized armies with futuristic graphics, secret agents' equipment and identity papers, progressing to more peaceful fantasies as the years passed by.

When the last big David Hicks office closed in 1991, part of its design archive went to the Victoria & Albert Museum, where it became part of the National Archive of Design. In a dusty warehouse in Olympia lie seventeen boxes of miscellaneous sketches, presentation drawings and fabric samples. These have yet to be properly catalogued, and when I first went to look at them, in 2000, I was struck by a mention in the list of their contents of 'sundry design sketches by David Hicks including an intercontinental ballistic missile'. This unexpected item turned out to be part of my fantasy army, drawn secretly at the back of some dreary classroom, sent to my father, and years later inadvertently included in the archive.

The Education of an Architect

I was about 13 when I started to design fantasy palaces rather than weapons, and here I was given huge encouragement by my father, who was thrilled at the prospect of an amenable, future architectural partner, having suffered for years from working with architects who were unable to grasp his furnishing needs and who would inevitably put doors in the wrong place. For a couple of years I worked away at a growing portfolio of buildings that were entirely 'DH' in inspiration. These were mainly rather streamlined and modern, with a lot of smoked glass and limestone, but with elaborate classical porticoes of Corinthian columns. My father would show them with great pride to visiting designers.

Ten years later, he would descend on my dingy student room in an ugly Victorian house in the country near Bath, and sweep me off to look at nearby gems like Lacock Abbey, with its ravishing Gothic Revival hall. Often we would go with my mother to Paris, to celebrate the opening of new room-sets at the David Hicks shop. We would go to Hubert de Givenchy's house for a drink and inspect his extraordinary eighteenth-century gunmetal furniture, and out to Versailles for the most private of private tours, going up on to the roof to look at the sculptures, and to the attic to see the hole in the little window overlooking the Cour de Marbre through which

My father posing in his studio with one of his torn-paper floral designs and the ever-present accessory, a cigarette.

Aeroflot offices, London, 1975, designed by my father with a vast photomural of Red Square and a red carpet.

James Fairfax's guest room, Sydney, 1976.

My picture of my father, mother and his French associate Christian Badin at Versailles, France, 1983.

David Hicks on decoration

The first of eleven books, 1966: 'Interior decoration is the art of achieving the maximum with the minimum'.

Opposite: Pamela, Edwina, India (kissing Bertie), David and Ashley Hicks at Britwell, 1970; a letter from Burma with sketched lacquer shopping; a page from the 1975 scrapbook; my childhood bed; and two of my father's strange drawings of his ever-growing empire.

the fat, shy King Louis XVI would poke his spyglass to peep at arriving dignitaries as they approached the palace.

My father was always a great one for trips and for 'seeing things'. His excitement at finding a new treasure to look at was enormous. He was indefatigable in this, often driving for hours for a glimpse of good plasterwork. He was always inordinately proud of having been, at the age of 17, the 'youngest ever member' of the Georgian Group, a society that organized visits to architecturally distinguished country houses. Wherever we were, if he should catch sight of what he called 'good trees', or glimpse the top of an obelisk or other monument, we would be off on one of his 'magical mystery tours', usually driving up to some complete stranger's house, where we were often summarily dismissed but occasionally rewarded with a new find.

In all of this, I was the child taken along and very consciously educated to understand what he was looking at. My sisters somehow elected at an early age to avoid all of this, and their complaints of tired feet in museums still echo in my head when I take my own girls out to look at things. Both Edwina and India inherited a great deal of style and creativity from my father, but are a little lost when it comes to dating a chair or a snuffbox. They were encouraged, as I was, to look at everything, to follow his work, and especially to share his passion for colour, but he, in his old-fashioned way, never expected or wanted his daughters to be anything but amateurs, while his son was naturally expected to succeed him in a design dynasty.

'I won't interfere at all'

It was therefore quite natural for him to ask me to write something about his life before it ended. Nothing came of it then, beyond my recording some of his earlier memories, but the seed was sown. Three years later I was overwhelmed by the level of interest in his work, and by frantic appeals by designers for David Hicks books, all out of print for many years. It seemed to me then (and even more so today) that, rather than simply reproducing those early books, in which so many glorious colour schemes are poorly rendered in grainy black and white, I should put together a new book using our archive of colour transparencies, in order to do proper justice to his career.

I intended to write a dry, objective text to go with these images, and of course was swayed by emotion and nostalgia towards something more like the 'Life' that he had always wanted to see written. My father told me at the start of our short-lived project that, 'If you make a statement and I don't agree with it, I'll just say, "Okay, fine, that's just the way you interpret it." It'll be no worse than some woman, too intrigued by me as a man (because I suppose I am sort of attractive to them)… They get carried away by all that and can't cut through it. That's what you must do. I won't interfere at all.'

Now, of course, he cannot interfere. Neither, sadly, can he finally see his life, or this brief outline of it, in print. It is merely an outline, and not the biography that he wanted. It is a picture book, a review of my father's work, concentrating on his strongest period, that which today has the most interest and influence for designers. The text is organized not chronologically but by subjects, so that after a look at my father's childhood and early influences we leap forward to Britwell (our own house, his best work) and then to consider the influence that travel had on him, and so on. My words are extremely personal, inevitably, since I am his son after all, and if I have made statements that readers do not agree with, all I can do is to repeat his own phrase, that it is just the way I interpreted it.

The Library of Memories

My father's library at The Grove, to which we moved from neighbouring Britwell in 1980, bears his imprint so clearly that it still, after four years, feels as if he is just getting himself another drink and will be back at any moment to show you his latest press cuttings in the newest of his black scrapbooks. There is the old mahogany partners' desk, the fax machine that he used the night before his death, his coloured pencils all nicely sharp and ready. There are postcards of the house, writing paper, a smattering of stiff, crested envelopes pinched from one royal residence or another, a white marble bust of young Prince Leopold and a photograph of his mother as a young bride. He had wanted at one stage to have all his books bound in red leather, and when this proved impossibly expensive he would wrap the spines of offensive-coloured books with odd pieces of old red damask or plain scarlet paper.

The morocco leather surface of the desk is completely worn through, right to the bare wood, where his wrists rubbed it night after night while drawing and writing his innumerable postcards and faxes. On it stands his grandfather's 1860 clock, a heavy Victorian object in black marble surmounted by an ormolu sphinx. He described this clock as summing up his background completely, 'redolent of the things my father inherited from his father, who probably bought everything', having made a little money stockbroking in the City. He traced the progress of his own life through the movements of this clock from his father's dining-room chimney, to the little houses that he shared with his mother, until it 'recovered its posture when I put it over the fireplace in my dressing-room bathroom at Britwell in 1961'.

He loved this clock so much that when he secured a particularly large contract for a small Southampton joinery firm with which he had worked for many years, and they offered to make him something out of gratitude, he chose to have a dwarf bookcase made following the clock's tapered, rusticated Egyptian form. The bookcase stands next to his desk in the same room, holding large books elaborately bound in scarlet leather, a mixture of albums holding his own pictures of beautiful objects and his design sketches for the house and the garden, and a three-volume set of Lutyens' work, including his Viceroy's House in New Delhi. My mother's links with India (as Lady Pamela Mountbatten, she was living in splendour at Viceroy's House while my father suffered in the army) were thus woven together with his design interests.

Atop this bookcase he placed a leather box labelled 'Hon Evelyn Ashley', which once held the correspondence of Evelyn's father, Lord Shaftesbury, the great Victorian reformer, whom he served as political secretary. Evelyn was my mother's great-grandfather, but my father, typically, stuffed the box with his own family things, old letters from Hickses long forgotten, yellowing 1890s school reports and bits of cloth from old Hicks evening dresses. In a drawer in the front of the box, after my father died, I found a poignant bundle of things of his brother's, including a small envelope pitifully inscribed, 'Things found in John's wallet when he was killed' (in Italy, near Assisi, in World War II), among which were pictures of John in his smart, new uniform, with little David staring up at him wide-eyed with admiration.

The linking and weaving-together of my mother's family and his, the appropriation of her far more glamorous background to clothe his world, was something that slowly grew on him. He delighted in her family history and connections – and in arranging and rearranging the various possessions that she had inherited – but he was also fiercely proud of his own few family things and never

for one moment tried to conceal his own quite ordinary origins. He would describe his village childhood in Essex, and his father's daily train journey to his City stockbroking office, with nothing but humour at the contrast between his childhood and my mother's.

My father's attachments to objects were quite extraordinary. They probably stemmed in part from the early traumas of having his father and brother die within a year of each other, which left 14-year-old David and his mother alone and somewhat impoverished in wartime England. (His father's stockbroking business had been put in charge of a cousin, who promptly lost everything.) They then faced the indignity of a house sale, selling everything that would not fit in the very much smaller house to which they moved. For my grandmother Iris, who had lost her first son twenty years before, all she was left with was to spoil little David rotten. For him, the trauma left an obsession with possessions, with collecting, with arranging his objects, with controlling everything around him.

What these objects and possessions have, apart from their intrinsic beauty, is a grain of memory and history. They are vessels of a rich, deep nostalgia that was just as much a part of him as his design talent. By the time I was asking him about his childhood, looking for influences that might have started him on the way to creating the interiors in this book, he was moving more and more in this nostalgic, elaborate fantasy world of memory and history. He loved to reach back for those images of a long-lost childhood, glimpses of houses, rooms and people like stepping stones along the way, each helping to form his style.

'What a pace you go, my boy'
Herbert Hicks had died when my father was only 12. He told me that it made little impression on him, since his father had been so old – in his seventies then – that he had barely known him. When he was 40, Herbert had married Iris Platten, the much younger daughter of his stockbroking partner. A first son had died aged 6, and it took years for Iris Hicks to persuade her husband to cease mourning the loss and have more children. When they did, he was always distant from them, as if fearing that they, too, would be taken from him.

Herbert was, by all accounts, a stylish figure, immaculately dressed always, with a fresh carnation in his buttonhole for his daily railway journey to the City. He was entirely Victorian in outlook, and his young wife never dared ask if she could take the acting lessons in London that she longed for. Instead she would walk him to the station, see him off on his train to London Bridge and secretly catch the next one herself five minutes later. She studied for years at the same school as John Gielgud. When Herbert's return train arrived in the evening, his dutiful wife would be there to greet him, full of village gossip, having in fact just managed to catch the previous train down from London herself.

Acting was considered all right if unpaid, so she formed the Hicksonians, an amateur dramatic society that put on one big production every year. The last of these, just before the War started and changed everything, was *The Lady with the Lamp*, the story of Florence Nightingale. Iris believed that the famous nurse was a distant relation and named her second son David Nightingale Hicks, only for him to discover that they had no connection at all and that he had endured years of schoolboy taunts for nothing. He was tremendously excited about the play, however, in which he had a tiny part, a young officer with one line to say. When the big night came, he was sick with flu and forced to stay in bed, missing his big chance – 'the great tragedy of my life', he called it.

He did remember clearly the huge excitement of the production, put on in their local theatre, with 'proper footlights and scenery, all designed by Mama and made by

My father in his library at The Grove, 1995, at his desk (on which stands his grandfather's 1860 clock).

1941: 12-year-old David with his brother John, who was off to the War (to be killed three years later, near Assisi).

Iris Hicks in jaunty mood and country tweeds, 1944, with the delivery van that she drove during the War.

Herbert Hicks, 1910, with an especially magnificent buttonhole on his Victorian suit, not a carnation for once.

A precocious, 12-year-old David Nightingale Hicks in a studio portrait for his mother, after his father's death.

Young David plays soldier on a family picnic near their Essex village home, with a cousin and Iris, right.

Birkin the builder at considerable expense. All the costumes were specially made by Miss Camp, the dressmaker.' These costumes remained for years in a huge dressing-up cupboard, and he recalled that they 'did make one conscious of fabric'. All those wonderful old velvets, bits of lace and braid, lying in a cupboard in wartime, clothes-rationed Britain, where even the royal family dressed in government-issue green wool, must have been a potent escape for an artistic child. Iris also made endless patchwork quilts, which were in fact absolutely hideous, but all the other village ladies thought she was very dashing because she used very bright colours and unexpected things.

While Herbert was busy breeding exotic orchids in an enormous greenhouse (he regularly won prizes at the London Orchid Show) and dressing up in Freemason's finery as Master of his local lodge, Iris was one of the great characters of the local social scene. She was notorious for her splendid sense of humour, and especially loved to tease any pretentious neighbours. She once dressed up as a gypsy woman and appeared at the front door of a particularly unsympathetic and snobbish local lady, offering to tell her fortune if she would 'cross me palm with silver, dearie…' and only revealing her identity when the haughty woman had thoroughly embarrassed herself.

Already when his father and brother were still alive, young David was spoiled terribly by his mother, who simply adored him. When he was at prep school, at the age of 8 or 9, she thought he should have a suit for the occasional, but rather grand, children's parties in the nearby town of Earl's Colne. She therefore had her tailor make him a dinner jacket ('Sadly it was so showy and people laughed so much…'). My father would go every three weeks to Mr Rogers for fittings for suits and jackets, and got to choose his own tweeds. He told me with great satisfaction, sixty years later, that 'I don't think many other people in England at that age chose their own tweeds and had their coats made to measure!'

My father's two clear memories of his own father were of the old man seated at his breakfast table, watching his young son hurtle around the dining room on a little bicycle, damaging all the furniture, merely saying, 'What a pace you go, my boy', and going on reading *The Times*; and then his last sight of him, as Iris drove him to the station to go back to school. Herbert was at the door, waving goodbye, while young David ignored him, chatting away with his mother, who abruptly stopped the car and made him turn and wave goodbye, saying, 'Look at your father, wave to him. You never know when you're going to see him again.' He never did see him again.

Early Artistic Experiments

Late one evening in 1941 at Charterhouse, his dread public school, 12-year-old D. N. Hicks was summoned by his housemaster, who told him, 'I've got some very sad news for you, Hicks, I'm afraid. Your father died this morning. Your mother particularly wanted me to tell you that there's nothing to worry about and she'll be coming to collect you, to take you home for a few days, but the funeral is tomorrow and she didn't think that you'd like to

be there.' My father barely knew what a funeral was at this age, although he did remember an occasion, when he was even smaller, how all the dark-red holland blinds had to be pulled down on the windows on the road and front sides of the house. Asking the maid the reason for this, he had been told that 'It's for the Colonel's funeral; the cortège is going past soon.' He later told me that this had rather intrigued him.

When his mother came to collect him from school, she was 'all smiles', as if nothing had happened. His brother John, then 19, was home on leave from the army, his last leave before going out to Africa and then Italy (where he died). John had already moved into their father's room, in which he had died, which their mother thought a good idea (they had slept in separate rooms), and had taken over his clothes. For young David, the apparition of his much older brother suddenly playing his father's role – even dressing the part – must have been even more confusing than the unseen removal of the old man from his life. He remembered it as 'great fun – like a holiday', with John trying on all of their father's outfits and taking David off to local pubs on his motorbike.

When John left, David was given the run of their suddenly empty house by his mother, who denied him nothing… ever. Money became a problem almost instantly, and both cars and live-in maids were let go, so my father was given the garage as a studio, the front spare room as a workshop and the back maids' bedroom as a painting studio. He clearly remembered bursting into tears of joy one afternoon when he discovered that, by putting vermilion, white and Naples yellow together, he could get a sort of skin colour. This was very exciting. He then made 'a horrific portrait of my mother, who looked absolutely witch-like'. He also began to experiment with interiors ideas – he took a plastic washing-up bowl, cut it in half and fixed the two pieces to the wall with lamps inside to make indirect lighting, which he 'thought frightfully smart'.

One evening, while they were at the cinema, a bomb destroyed Coggeshall church. The next day he went and poked around among the ruins, finding a thirteenth-century carved stone head, which he put up on the wall of his garage studio. Also during the War, Iris Hicks and her son used to raise money for the Royal Air Force. They would form a little *tableau vivant* on the back of their pony cart. Iris would dress up as Queen Elizabeth I, with David as Lord Essex and Sapsford the gardener leading the pony. They had a dulcitone on the cart and Iris played a few notes on that and then recited some great speech from Queen Elizabeth. About twenty-five people would stand around on the village green to watch – quite impromptu; they would just arrive – and then young David would go around with a collecting box. 'It did', he told me, 'make one not shy at all about standing up and talking in front of people, and good at projecting one's voice, which stood me in very good stead later on.'

First Influences

When I asked my father what had first inspired him to become a designer, what his earliest memories of glamour, of stylish houses and ways of living were, I was given a whole raft of images. As one of a group of schoolboys put there to wave, he had seen the King and Queen drive down the Long Walk from Windsor ('very glamorous indeed'). He often played truant from school football, going to the cinema near Charterhouse, watching endless Fred Astaire films – 'very luxurious, very glamorous, all those thirties interiors and the cigarette cases they tapped cigarettes on'. He was impressed by Sigmund Politzer, an artist who drew his portrait at Charterhouse in 1944, and his studio, in a cottage by the river. Politzer had very neat rows of boxes of Turkish cigarettes, 'enough to last the entire war. Everything was in profusion but all in immaculate order in a very small cottage. I suppose that was the first time I saw that immaculate attention to detail of any sort.'

He remembered new neighbours arriving in their village, lorry after lorry disgorging furniture and pictures and objects, causing great excitement, everyone longing to see who owned it all. The owner proved to be Italian: 'I don't think she was a very grand Italian, but she had style,

John Hicks off to a hunt, seen off by his mother and little David on his pony, in Essex, 1936.

John (in his Royal Horse Artillery uniform) with Iris at the door of The Hamlet, Coggeshall, May 1941.

Little David on his pony, 1936, with Iris, the mother who 'could never deny him anything... ever'.

Grown-up David after his National Service, with a proud Iris and a new suit, 1949.

Setting off to see yet more of the world with a rather improbable rucksack on his back, around 1950.

in a dress down to the ground and with her hair done very elaborately; we all realized that this was someone of some consequence. She really did look Edwardian.' The dining room had paintings of Paris at night, street scenes with tram cars. The whole house smelled of incense, with crucifixes everywhere. It was quite different to all the other houses in the village because it was not like a country house at all and had wall-to-wall carpeting everywhere.

You actually felt, he told me, that you could hardly sit down. The woman didn't really have any taste, but she had a powerful personality and a very strong way of making her house look. It was totally original, quite different and something he had never seen before. It had 'great atmosphere, great style', he said. 'It's not a style that I now would like, but I was intrigued.' It was intimidating and she was rather intimidating too, but she was very sweet to him, because he was polite and had such good manners. She liked his drawings, which he used to go and show her, encouraged by his mother, who never doubted that she had given birth to the new Michelangelo. The intimidating

quality of both house and owner was something that pervaded both my father's own houses and those that he did for clients, and the idea of a room so perfect that you were afraid to break the spell by sitting down or touching anything is very familiar to me from my own childhood.

His mother took him often to see Geoffrey Holme, who edited *The Studio* magazine and lived nearby, and had an enormous library crowded with books from floor to ceiling. In the middle of the room, on a table, was a huge model of an unbuilt project for a cathedral he had designed – which impressed his young visitor greatly. Holme had taken a small octagonal sitting room on the ground floor and painted it brilliant blue, using Ricketts' Blue, a blue powder hair rinse for elderly women which could make quite a good paint, with incredibly strong colour. He had taken oval, octagonal, circular and rectangular frames, mirrors, drawings and miniatures, then painted them white and massed them on the brilliant-blue walls. 'I thought that was absolute magic,' my father told me. 'I'd never seen anything like that before. The place had enormous style. It was the first decorated house I saw.'

David Hicks, the Clever Young Interior Decorator

Young David Hicks never ceased to rule his mother's life, and when in 1954, at the age of 25, he decided that he simply had to have a London house to decorate – for he was going to make a career of being a decorator – she immediately sold their half-timbered cottage in the country and the few remaining shares that her husband had left her, to buy the lease on 22 South Eaton Place. He had already (ten years before) chosen their new house, redecorated it, designed a garden, and generally made every decision, all with her willing acquiescence, so that she was now happily swept along with enthusiasm for the new scheme.

He had spent a short, unhappy time 'painting cereal packets' in the graphics studio of advertising agency J. Walter Thompson, after four years at the Central School of Art and Design. There he had studied everything from typography to theatre design, book illustration to painting, a varied, free-ranging course that was a perfect grounding for the career to come. He had travelled all over Europe, everywhere looking at great houses of the past and the present, his keen eye picking out every detail of their decoration and of the style of the lives lived within them. Gradually he was deciding that an artist he would never be, but as a decorator he could make a name for himself.

The house was a fairly typical late nineteenth-century one, just within chic Belgravia. The architect Clough Williams-Ellis had lived there thirty years before, which was the only interest that it had besides well-proportioned rooms and the occasional original chimneypiece. When he started on the project, my father had no idea where to get anything, but luckily had a friend working at Colefax & Fowler who gave him a list of their suppliers. It was so soon after the War that there was very little available, and he had to resort to things like felt for the floor. This, in fact, just made him even more adventurous in what he did.

There were no good patterned fabrics anywhere, besides endless floral chintzes. My father saw that John Fowler had firmly established the 'English Country House' look, and was determined to do his own thing rather than appear 'a mere copyist'. He discovered that Sanderson's and Coles still had their huge collections of printing blocks for wallpapers that had been unused for forty years or more. My father had some newly printed for the house: an Owen Jones design and a Pugin one, which were 'absolutely fantastic, scarlet background, khaki, black and brilliant yellow. It was a very, very good colourway. They were showstoppers.'

Conscious of needing to make a real impact, in a city where most houses were still drably decorated in 1930s eau de nil and grey, he made surprising, often bizarre, colour combinations the keynote. Each room was strikingly different, each contrived to make an instant impression of great strength. People were 'astounded, they were fascinated. They'd never seen anything like it before. It was, after all, 1954.' A hall with chalk-white wallpaper with a lime-green and rust Chinese design; white-painted hall chairs; just the way he hung the three pictures over the table – it said something and they paid attention. On the landing there sat a bright-yellow covered sofa, the frame painted dark green. It was a house of contrasts, featuring a black-and-white dining room and a grey drawing room with pictures all framed with different-coloured mounts.

When the house was absolutely, perfectly, immaculately complete – and not one moment before – he invited people to see it. He never had a big party, of course, because the house would not have looked at its best, its rooms crammed with people, his carefully composed walls hidden behind chattering guests. Instead, he would ask two or three at a time. He invited Peter Coats – then, and for many years afterwards, the Gardening Editor of *House & Garden* – who returned with a photographer from the magazine the very next day. The photographs were so good that Peter told him to telephone Mrs Rex Benson (she had been Mrs Condé Nast), who was looking for a decorator. She was delighted. 'Oh,' she said, 'I'm just so bored with everyone else, it all looks the same, I've had Syrie Maugham and John Fowler and Billy Baldwin; now I'd like you!'

Peter also introduced him to Maureen Dufferin, whose dining-room chairs he covered in 'frightfully expensive pure silk damask'; to Mrs Douglas Fairbanks, who began by asking for two cushions for her summer house but went on quickly to bigger things; and to Chips Channon and his son, Paul, for whom he worked for many years (so many that Paul, now Lord Kelvedon, proudly declared in his address at my father's memorial service in London that he had 'slept in a David Hicks bedroom for over forty years'). They all sent him on to yet others, and soon, as he told me, 'everyone was talking about David Hicks, the clever young interior decorator. Don't let's deny that being extremely good-looking was a very great asset. There are, or were, very few ugly, successful interior decorators; there are quite a lot now, perhaps, but then it was considered to be rather an advantage.'

22 South Eaton Place: the study with bright-red walls, an armchair from Eaton Hall and curtains in blue felt.

The grey drawing room, including massed pictures with multicoloured mounts over a vermilion sofa with green trim.

Christmas Greetings from David Hicks

A Christmas card featuring my father's sketch of his house.

A World of its Own

Britwell, our country house in Oxfordshire, was my whole world as a child. There were other houses: our small London house, our holiday homes in France and the Bahamas; my grandfather's house in Hampshire, his castle in Ireland and my cousins' house in Kent; and a dread succession of dreary school houses. The schools were the opposite of home, and although I am sure they were much nicer than they could have been, there was never any possibility of feeling properly at home in them. Holidays were just that, while London was for one-night visits to the dentist, theatre and museums. Home was Britwell.

It was like a world, too — an ideal, isolated world of impossible beauty, cut off from everything outside its gates by a long drive beyond which I was not allowed to go until I was old enough to bicycle down to the village alone. Until then I roamed the woods around the house, lurked in the garden in some military guise or other, or stayed inside. Being a bookish, introverted child, I did a great deal of staying indoors. Once I had left for boarding school, my time at home was very precious and I would be everywhere in the house, inwardly claiming every inch as my own, wandering possessively through the rooms, cataloguing to myself their contents, their designs.

The house was not huge, but it was big, especially for one that has just been entirely redecorated. Each room being in a markedly different style exaggerated its size. In reality it is a medium-sized mansion built in three stages from 1728 to 1790. All in red brick, with dressings of local stone, it has a central block linked to symmetrical wings by curving passages, with an oval chapel set behind one of them. The chapel, with elaborate Baroque plasterwork, was added for the Catholic owners in 1760. Together with the stone hall and high staircase hall to one side, this gives the house an air of architectural importance that belies its size.

It was these features — coupled with an imposing, stone memorial column in front of the house, an obelisk in the park and the wonderful vista of rolling hills in which it sits — that sold Britwell to my parents in 1960. They had not intended to buy a country house, having not yet finished decorating their small London apartment, and certainly not anything on such a scale. My father spotted, quite by chance, a small advertisement in *The Times* with a picture of Britwell's perfect façade, 'for sale with 200 acres'. They were just back from their honeymoon, having arrived to find that my grandmother, Edwina Mountbatten, had died in Borneo, and driving my mother down to Oxfordshire to see a possible house seemed like a fine distraction from her grief.

Buying the house was a still better distraction, but there were other motives. Just as decorating and publishing his house in South Eaton Place had launched my father's career, it was obvious that a house on the scale of Britwell would give endless potential for productive publicity. His visits to houses like Yves Vidal's York Castle in Tangier, Wright Luddington's in Santa Barbara and Rory Cameron's La Fiorentina on Cap Ferrat gave him an idea of the kind of impact that lavish, modern styling might have on an old house in the English countryside. The use of York Castle as a setting for Knoll furniture was especially instructive, although the subtle blend of old and new which already constituted the 'David Hicks style' would be even more photogenic.

Early Days, a Spare Aesthetic

Immediately after buying the house, my father went on a lecture tour to Australia, invited by the famous department store David Jones to speak to a thousand Australian housewives on the art of decoration. While

My grandfather, slightly dismayed by the thoroughness of his son-in-law's 'decoration' of Britwell, 1961.

The hall at Britwell, 1963, with the severe Baroque chimney and plasterwork that first attracted my father.

My mother in the drawing room at Britwell, 1965, in front of the elaborately carved chimneypiece.

there, he began to sketch design solutions to Britwell's main rooms. These sketches are fluid and painterly, rather Baroque in feeling, and quite unlike his later graphic, precise style of unerring black lines. The Baroque style extends to a series of garden plans of great avenues radiating out from the house in every direction, with a grandeur of scale that would have made it the Marly of Oxfordshire, had they been planted. The interior sketches are far more practical, and show him mulling over furnishing and wall treatments in his usual detailed way.

He began quite self-consciously, aiming at a look of spare, empty elegance inspired by paintings of the early eighteenth century, interiors by Hogarth, Zoffany and Arthur Devis, with barely furnished interiors of the same sort of date as Britwell's architecture. This was, of course, eminently practical for a large house, and for my parents, who had almost no furniture. The look was also quite novel in a country house. Almost all houses at the time still had their Victorian decoration, crowded with objects and furniture of every conceivable style, tiger-skin rugs and regimental flags, armies of tiny tea tables and yards of white cretonne. Styles of life had changed dramatically, but not, in most cases, the interiors in which these lives were lived. A few houses had been modernized in the Lutyens, Arts and Crafts tradition before 1914, and a few more in the Syrie Maugham, Oliver Hill way between the wars, but since then almost nothing had happened.

A very few stylish, artistic types had made small attempts at a cleaner look, but generally the results were fussy and dull. Certainly there was nothing modern about them. England is remarkable in the world for having so much of its artistic wealth wrapped up in its country houses, quite unlike most European countries, where creativity was concentrated in centralized court circles or in cities. As a result, the English country house is not only the repository of the bulk of our national cultural heritage;

it is also an international style icon. Especially since the destruction, in the first decades of the twentieth century, of most of the grand London houses, the English country house has come to occupy a unique place in the world, as witnessed by the popularity of the 'English Country House' look in American decorating.

The look, though, had nothing new about it in 1960. The houses were stodgy and old-fashioned. The few new houses were dolls'-house versions of the old, and the even fewer modern ones were not country houses at all but suburban villas transplanted into a rural setting. What was totally lacking was any revitalized house in the great tradition of Blenheim, Belvoir or Boughton, with a modern look that embraced the past and mixed new and old in a fresh, exciting way. My father told me that, in the 1950s, 'I would go to any country house that I could possibly worm my way into during those formative years. I think I learned a very great deal about architecture and about style, furniture and living just by doing that, by seeing so many different houses.'

So it was that he came to decorate and begin to live in Britwell in 1960–61 in a totally new way, and to create there a look particularly his own. To begin with, that look was very like what he had been doing in the four years before marriage, when he had absorbed influences from Californian decorating, from Wright Luddington and from friends like Tony Hail in San Francisco. This was a relaxed, easy style of off-white walls, blond wood, beige fabrics, with antiques and modern furniture mixing happily together. The look was, in fact, not unlike the prevailing style of today.

The Grand Style of Mr Hicks

In his own living room in South Eaton Place, in 1957, my father had removed all the colour that had made such an effective splash in 1954's *House & Garden*, replacing the

My father in his London drawing room, 1958, newly redecorated, after California, in off-white and beige.

heavily carved, gilt vastness of his armchair from Victorian Eaton Hall with the latest modern, Danish chairs by Poul Kjaerholm. Out went the purple, magenta, lilac and vermilion; in came tone on tone of beige, parchment, ivory and black. Out went the wall crowded with tiny pictures in different-coloured mounts, and in their place came bare walls and a Sidney Nolan drawing on a small stand. Having made the splash, now he needed sophistication and easy elegance, a fresh, modern look.

In the same spirit, he had decorated Vidal Sassoon's first married home in 1958, a small apartment on an even smaller budget, before Sassoon became one of the world's most famous hairdressers. This was again mainly white, with two Louis XV fauteuils flanking a severe modern table. To balance a window, he created a similarly white-curtained bookshelf alcove; the books were so ugly that he covered every one with white cartridge paper. Sassoon was thrilled with the result, and they went on to collaborate on his first Bond Street salon.

While the look of the rooms at Britwell was spare and empty, the style of life there was not. Money seemed no object at the time, and butlers, footmen, chefs and housekeepers were recruited to run the place. My father, interviewing a particularly imposing potential butler, could think of no good butler-interview question beyond 'Are you very strong? We will be moving the furniture about a good deal', which produced a Jeeves-like raised eyebrow. The extensive hothouses were under the aegis of a Fellow of the Royal Horticultural Society, who bred the most exotic blooms including – miracle of miracles – bananas that fruited in Oxfordshire!

Some of these excesses were corrected quite early on, as when the accountant came to lunch and, presented with one of the famous Britwell bananas as his dessert, cut it into five equal pieces, popping each into his mouth with the words, 'Each piece, £10.' The hothouses were closed,

the RHS Fellow went elsewhere and the banana tree moved into the hall, where it stood always in my childhood, slightly forlorn-looking, doubtless wistful for its fruitful youth. As my father described it, 'although we had lived in a pretty grand way in the early 1960s, right from the outset I had tried to be practical. I had, for instance, installed a house telephone so that we could ring the groom to say when we wanted to go riding.'

This internal telephone had twenty-one extensions, including, rather improbably, one for the 'Gardens'. Anyone who came to stay for the weekend, and very many people did, would be called by my father half an hour after their breakfast had been brought to them, proposing the plan for the day, the tour of the estate, the visit to the thirteenth-century almshouses at nearby Ewelme, and so on. It was hectic at times, between cultural excursions, riding, tennis and swimming in the large pool and, of course, the very lengthy and detailed tour of the house itself. This would take at least a couple of hours, often followed by the guest being settled down in the library with a drink and the latest of my father's black scrapbooks.

The style of the house was an extraordinary mixture. Lunch might be in the low, panelled breakfast room, understated and rustic in feeling, all oatmeal and cream colours, with naive nineteenth-century jugs on brackets, a scrubbed pine table and a long bench seat, while dinner in the dining room was a blaze of silver and gold on crisp white linen laid over the rich, scarlet damask cloth. The dining room was very large, with its domed plasterwork ceiling resplendent with symbols of the Mass. Each place was set with a different gold beaker for water, and a different gold box full of cigarettes for anyone who wanted (like their host) to smoke throughout the meal. The rug, laid on the smooth, stone floor, was scarlet felt, with a dark-brown border, while the butler wore a complementary outfit of dark brown with a scarlet collar.

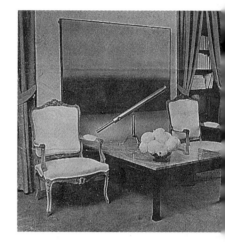

Vidal Sassoon's apartment, 1958. The curtained bookcase with cartridge-paper book jackets is on the right.

The banana tree, forlorn and fruitless in the hall at Britwell after the hothouses were closed, 1968.

The Britwell dining room with its magnificent domed plasterwork ceiling, built as a Catholic chapel in 1760.

Edwina and I in our night nursery at Britwell. My horse tricycle was French, 1880.

My bedroom, Britwell, 1970, with sheets in the 'H'-logo pattern that covers this book.

The World's Largest Showroom

'I was determined that it would not be an interior decorator's showpiece', my father said. 'I did not want the rooms to look like overdramatic or unnecessarily photogenic showrooms.' This was our home, and it was a cosy, warm, family house. That said, as children we were mainly kept to our top-floor nursery, brought down to be shown off at tea, polished and arranged rather like the massed objects that were so carefully shown in his 'tablescapes'. The objects themselves were for us to look at but not touch, as we were always reminded ('Those are Daddy's toys; yours are in the nursery'), but we were expected to take a serious interest in them. We all remember to this day the huge pride we would feel if one of our childish creations ever achieved the immortal status of inclusion in one of the tablescapes.

My father was always proud of having 'invented tablescapes' or, at any rate, having been the first not only to assemble these still-life compositions but to give them their catchy name. Today, every decorating book talks about them, and much is made of the art of putting objects together, but since I do not believe the word was used before he wrote it in *David Hicks on Living – with Taste*, he was right to claim credit. He saw the same thing done by many people (among them his adored Winnifreda, Countess of Portarlington), and told me that 'Winnie had this immaculate thing, this way of arranging objects, everything absolutely in order, which is rather where I got it from.' He saw similar things at Chips Channon's house, at Rory Cameron's, in many places, but it was Earlywood, the Portarlingtons' house at Ascot, which really inspired him. He loved that house, with its tables crammed with wonderful gold boxes and objects, and the vast jardinières containing flowers in bloom brought in from the hothouses.

For all his reverence for precious objects, my father got just as much pleasure from quite ordinary things that he found beautiful, be they old bits of driftwood, shells or cheap plastic boxes. When he was younger, he would make marvellous tablescapes, mixing precious and ordinary to great effect. At 60, he was always reinventing everything around him, making new things out of old.

He was excited by the contrast of rich objects and poor, like a fine ormolu *Directoire* incense burner placed on a rough, terracotta flowerpot dish turned upside down, or an exquisite pair of eighteenth-century Chinese porcelain birds sitting on a base which he had collaged with cut-up photographs of greenery torn from magazines, the type scribbled out with black pen.

The nursery was by no means the least decorated part of Britwell. By the time naughty little India Hicks was old enough to mess up the decoration of her room, she did so with posters and stickers and the like, whereas my older sister Edwina and I never for a moment considered making our rooms any less perfect than he had left them. Mine was decorated in 1970, using David Hicks sheets from American textile giant Stevens Utica, bold stripes stuck to walls and ceiling suggestive of a Regency campaign tent. Bed and chairs were done over in military khaki from my grandfather's tailor, edged in scarlet like an army officer's drill uniform. The scheme was arranged entirely for my pleasure and benefit, but of course could never be changed. I still feel a chill remembering the dreadful day when, working on a tank model, I spilled green enamel paint on one of the expensively covered chairs.

Being my father's house, his controlling hand was everywhere. Every room was design perfection, but also totally lived in and comfortable (if not, perhaps, very relaxing). It was all rather like the Italian neighbour's house

My father's bathroom. He kept a rifle by the loo, and shot grey pigeons from the windows, sparing the doves.

he remembered from his own childhood, as though under a spell of perfection that might be broken if anything was moved. He himself, of course, could (and did) move everything all the time, constantly arranging and rearranging objects, pictures and, to a lesser extent, furniture. Unlike most designers' homes, however, which are often slightly chaotic and unfinished, with visible signs of progress and development, his was always completely perfect at any given moment. He might have rearranged the whole room the night before, but it would always look as though every piece was in its only conceivable place.

The scale of the house was such that when, in 1973, he wanted to create a new, very modern living room and some extra guest bedrooms, he could do so in a wing that had been decorated ten years before but not much used. The excitement of the new Long Room, with walls of pink felt and fabrics, carpets and pictures of clashing reds and pinks, was enormous, not least for its surprising location in an eighteenth-century country house. The press coverage of the new room was huge, and the new David Hicks shops in Paris, Brussels and London all benefitted greatly from this and from the new look that the rooms defined. I was old enough to take a real interest in the project and was hugely proud of this wild and unexpected interior.

Part of the intention of the Long Room was to have somewhere for my father to listen to Wagner played very loud. While the connection between the music and the decor was not immediately obvious, I well recall the thrill of listening to the powerful, swelling waves of *Götterdämmerung* in that strange, fiery world of red on red, with its eclectic mix of scarlet-lacquer 1720 chairs and modern stainless steel. With a ceiling of acoustic tiles, cut off in the wing far from the rest of the house, he would turn the volume up so high that the big American ice cubes in his gin and tonic would tremble against the sides of the glass.

The Long Room was more like a showroom than any other in the house – partly, of course, because it served no real, obvious purpose besides late-night Wagner. In another way, though, it was one of the clearest expressions of my father's philosophy of living in the country at that time, and gave him possibly more satisfaction than any other room in the house. To a great extent, the entire house was in reality a showroom, despite his professed avoidance of such a thing. It was a showroom on a scale that no designer attempted before or since, and achieved huge results in publicity terms as well as giving tremendous satisfaction to him personally.

Two peacocks at Britwell, 1969. My father, from the steps, watches one of the decorative birds go by.

Second book, 1968 – 'Living with taste, good or bad, affects us all in every detail'.

A Night at Britwell

Britwell was the fullest expression of my father's style and was for eighteen years both his laboratory and his showroom. In his first five *David Hicks on…* books, a great number of the pictures are of rooms at Britwell, or details thereof. It was a defining fact of his life in those vital, productive, creative years. He would travel the world consulting, advising, designing for clients who had been wooed by pictures of the famous house. Others would be invited down for a night, and from their first glimpse of the

beautiful red-brick façade sitting gracefully in its little valley below them as they came over the brow of Britwell Hill they were totally seduced. Driving up to the house, its wings stretching out in a lazy embrace, they would be lost.

I like to imagine arriving there, as a stranger, for the night. There would be my father, maybe in a grey suit just down from London, climbing out of his chocolate-brown Rolls-Royce, or in country tweeds getting down from his Land Rover with 'Britwell Salome Estate' printed neatly on

The breakfast room, a low, panelled room, left deliberately rustic (in contrast to the dining room).

Three impossibly perfect little children, arranged like objects in a tablescape – Edwina, India and Ashley, 1970.

Theseus or Perseus, posing on a stone urn, the Simeon memorial column behind.

The Swedish room, whose bathroom door was cut through the painting seen next to the splendid bed.

The Octagon room, Britwell, complete with an octagonal Hicks carpet.

the doors and his 'H'-logo flag flying in front, his faithful shooting dog Bertie at his heels, every inch the country gentleman. Into the hall we would go, where a fire roars in the splendid stone hearth or, in summer, great baskets of newly cut roses wait fragrantly, ready for the magician to work his magic (see *David Hicks on Flower Arranging* for further details).

The butler, immaculate in his livery, takes care of the bags as we go into the drawing room for a moment. There we find my mother getting up from the sofa, her little Dachshund scampering at her feet. After a few minutes, in troop three impossibly perfect little children, shepherded in by a young, fresh-faced nanny in smart nursery uniform, greeting the new arrival with all the juvenile politeness of the English. We go through to the breakfast room for tea, where deliciously butter-sodden, hot crumpets are produced, with my father's favourite Australian Vegemite and a rich fruitcake. The silver napkin rings make a very particular noise on the rough, scrubbed pine table.

Outside the window, the ground is mid-height to the room, and a splendid male peacock appears, surreally floating, slowly and proudly fanning his wonderful tail feathers and then gravely turning to show them off to maximum effect. The children argue about whether this is Theseus or Perseus (are your own peacocks not named after heroes from Greek mythology?), while my mother gracefully pours more tea from the Georgian silver teakettle, with its little flame below to keep it properly hot. After tea, we go up to our room – the Swedish Room (named, we are immediately told, after the Swedish Empire furniture, gifts from the late Queen of Sweden). We are shown the bathroom, luckily, since its door is concealed in the panelling and has a large Victorian painting hung right across it. Picture and frame are both cut straight through to give access to the bathroom ('Not much of a picture,' our host explains.)

After a delicious hot bath – for there is none of that fabled English country-house discomfort here – we go down to find our host at his desk in the library, dictating captions for his latest book into a small Dictaphone. He takes us through to the Octagon room, next to the drawing room, where he pours out drinks and starts the newest Burt Bacharach record playing on the huge wood-cased hi-fi. The elaborate, High Gothic chimneypiece is missing – gone to an exhibition of the period in Brighton, and replaced temporarily by a life-size, enlarged photograph of the engraving of its design in Batty Langley's book of 1742. In the drawing room, my father gets out one of the huge photograph albums from their purpose-built cases with python-skin tops that sit between the windows. The album, filled with oversized prints of his own pictures of churches in Ethiopia, is covered in African woven cloth that he found there.

So it goes on, the evening continuing, the weekend unfolding, and each moment carefully, elaborately stage-managed to achieve aesthetic perfection, every tiny prop precisely in place. All the while, my mother is quietly, gracefully, in the background, talking interestingly about the latest biography, or of her impressions of Martin Luther King when she met him while staying with Nehru in India, or perhaps telling some amusing family story on cue from my father, who otherwise noisily dominates the whole proceedings, showing off his house, his family, his possessions, his world…

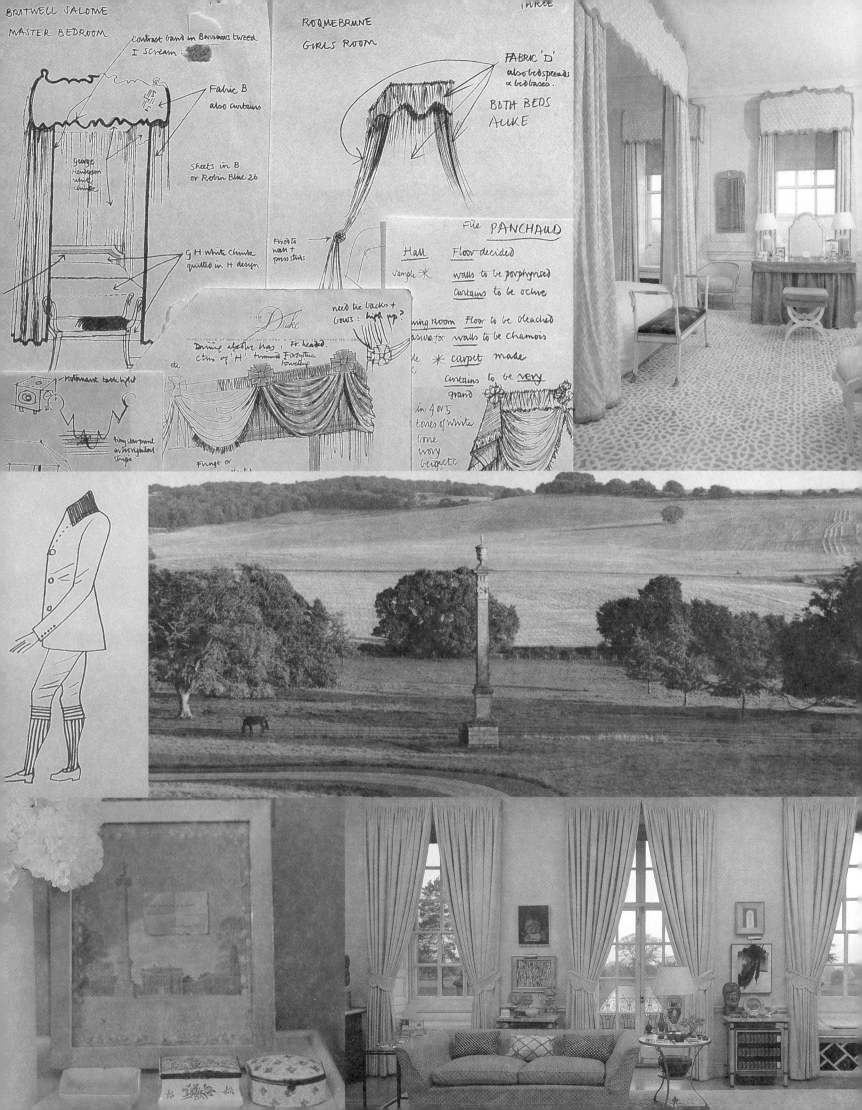

BRITWELL SALOME
MASTER BEDROOM

Contrast Grand in Barranza's tweed
I scream :

Fabric B
also curtains

George Henderson white chintz

Sheets in B
or Robin Blue 26

G H white chintz quilted in H design

ROQUEBRUNE
GIRLS ROOM

FABRIC 'D'
also bedspreads & bedbases.

BOTH BEDS
ALIKE

Fixers to wall + press studs

permanent table light.

tiny star pinl or strapplant stripe

THREE

The Drake
PARK AVENUE AT 56th STREET, NEW YORK, N.Y. 10022 · TELEPHONE HA 1-090

need the backs + Gours : high up?

Dining atelier has : Fr. headed.
Ctns of 'H' trimmed Forsythia toweling

Fringe or

File PANCHAUD

Hall   Floor decided
sample ✳   walls to be porphyrised
            Curtains to be ochre

Dining room Floor to be bleached
             for walls to be chamois
         ✳   carpet made
             Curtains to be very
             grand

in 4 or 5
tones of white
bone
ivory
beige etc

First Journey

My grandfather, Herbert Hicks, never slept on foreign shores. He once had to go to France on some family business, but luckily it was sufficiently near the Channel that he was able to go over on the morning boat and come back in the evening, so he could sleep both nights in some decent English establishment and not have to risk more than a quick lunch in dreaded France. He was of that generation of Englishmen who were not keen on foreigners – like King George V, whose secretary instructed the Foreign Office to arrange the royal train journey to Nice 'so far as possible to avoid meeting any Frenchmen'.

My grandmother Iris, instead, had travelled everywhere with her parents as a girl, and we still have her tour album, with its big plate photographs of Florence, Aden and Cairo. Herbert was her father's junior partner in the stockbroking firm, twenty years older than her, and very much set in his ways. She doubtless longed to travel, but could persuade him no further than Margate or Broadstairs. Her longing must have communicated itself to little David, however, and, just as soon as he was able, my father was off. The War was just ended, however, and it was difficult for him to go anywhere. In 1946, he had left his hated school, Charterhouse, and gone to London to attend the Central School of Art and Design.

One day at the Central, aged 17, halfway up the stairs, he saw a notice saying, 'Exchange Students: Does any student wish to make an exchange visit?' He rushed into the office and said, 'Yes, absolutely. What have you got?' They offered him a visit to a Pierre Buffière in Avignon, which they said was in the south of France. He agreed to go. That evening, he got back to where he was living – a rented room at the Grosvenor Chapel in South Audley Street – and promptly mentioned the exchange visit to Canon Ratcliffe, another lodger, who said, 'My dear child.

Avignon! The most wonderful city, the city of the popes! You must go!'

So off he went to Paris, waking on the train in the middle of Provence as the sun was coming up, suddenly seeing 'this Van Gogh landscape going by the window. It was intoxicating, absolutely intoxicating.' The visit lasted six weeks. Pierre's parents were dull; his father was a retired banker, 'a rather testy little man, an awful house full of mosquitoes, by the railway line'. But things soon looked up, for Pierre had a very pretty girlfriend, Nicole, and one day the English visitor was asked to go and play tennis with her, and discovered that she lived in a chateau on an island, just opposite the Papal Palace. So, of course, the next year he went back and stayed there instead of in Pierre's awful house, because her mother wanted her to learn English. As he told me with satisfaction, 'I never went back to 13, Avenue de la Treillade again in my entire life.'

It was marvellous, at the age of 17, to be in Provence. Imagine Avignon, not the way it is now, but a small, ancient city, almost entirely within the medieval walls. It was absolutely idyllic. He had a wonderful summer and he did learn a little French: 'It was so different, you see, from London, so different from Essex.' There was an extraordinary antique shop in the middle of the city, in a beautiful medieval house, run by 'two old queens'. They had wonderful things: there was a marvellous medieval courtyard at the back with a fountain dripping, dripping, dripping. He bought a set of coloured *Directoire* engravings, which he kept in one holiday house or other until he died. It was magic.

While there he was sketching, gouacheins, drawing away in black and white, careful line drawings of Nicole's mother's drawing room with a Louis XVI chair and an Empire commode, the Palais des Monnaies, the Palais des

Papes, churches… Then, at the end of the stay, they went to the Côte d'Azur, where they stayed in 'a rather nasty apartment' that the Buffières rented. It had bright-green wooden shutters, which they opened in the morning, to reveal a staggering view of the incredible 'blue, blue, blue' Mediterranean. About a hundred yards away was a delightful small hotel, which had been decorated in a very stylish way, slightly surrealist.

The whole thing was very chic and my father responded to it immediately: 'I suppose that every new thing, every new town, church, antique shop one saw gave one more and more fuel, ideas and excitement.' He was intrigued by that whole world. Nicole, who lived in the chateau, had an aunt who lived in Paris, so when next he was in Paris he stayed with 'Tante Claude', who was very sweet and lived with her mother, a charming old lady. There he was in the seventh arrondissement, highly comfortable, a perfectly nice lunch and dinner cooked for him. He could roam Paris with a good, stable base to go back to. 'That was a jolly fortunate thing,' he told me, 'but I've been a very fortunate man; I've had a very lucky life.'

The Grand Tour

After several summers in Provence, and after leaving the Central, my father was 22, with no particular career plan, thinking vaguely of becoming an artist. After years of poring over its art and architecture in books, it was finally time to see Italy for himself. He had a small Austin car and in this he set off to tour Italy. It was the Grand Tour of the eighteenth century, but not quite so grand. His intention was to make a whole portfolio of drawings as he went, in a very graphic style that he had developed at the Central, gouaches with strong, flat colour and the architectural lines outlined in white. His vague plan was to have an exhibition of these when he returned, which he was sure would be a sell-out success. He never did lack confidence.

The drawings, many of which we still have, are beautiful, although the show never happened. He did sell a few while in Italy, but all the same managed to run out of money in Venice after too many lunches at Harry's Bar. Luckily he met an English friend, who lent him enough to tide him over until his mother could send him out more, but there was an awkward week when he got stuck in Turin, imposing on the hospitality of an architect he had met in France the year before. The tour was a huge success, though, in that he saw everything he had ever wanted – Genoa, Rome, Naples, Capri, Sicily. He drew the Greek temples at Paestum and Segesta. He drew the Baptistry in Florence. He went to Vicenza and saw all of Palladio, even getting into the Villa Rotonda, which was, as he said, not easy in those days.

The excitement of this journey was tremendous. After years of dreaming, here he was. Everything about Italy was new and wonderful. Provence had been lovely but he knew it so well and, apart from the occasional Roman monument, the Musée Fragonard in Grasse, the old villages and Nicole's little chateau, there was little of real quality to look at. In Italy he did not know where to turn – the gardens, the houses, the towns, the ancient remains, churches and museums. On top of all this, there was the wonderful heat and sun, the exotic, beautiful people, the fabulous food. This was travelling, this was the world. The expensive visits to Harry's Bar gave him a glimpse of the glamorous international set and their lifestyle, which was every bit as exciting as the artistic treasures in the Accademia.

Most summers he returned to Provence, to the Côte d'Azur, to Venice. He saw famous Mexican millionaire aesthete Charles de Beistegui, as he wrote thirty years later, 'endlessly picnicking on the Lido beach at a damask-covered table with seventeenth-century style X-framed chairs…his house party waited on by uniformed footmen.

My father travelling in Italy, 1951, on his personal version of an English gentleman's Grand Tour.

One of my father's gouaches made in Italy, using vibrant colours, with the architecture outlined in crisp white.

My father posing in a leather coat on Charles de Beistegui's spiral column at the Chateau de Groussay, 1970.

Some of my father's travel photographs: a lunch party given by Teddy Millington-Drake at Villa Albrissi, 1961.

Birdcages and sun loungers beneath the deep arcades of Palladio's Villa Maser in the Veneto, Italy, 1961.

And one evening I saw him on his motorized barge, a Venetian sailor on the prow holding a paddle horizontally, when he took Don Juan (the Spanish pretender) down the Grand Canal to his Palazzo Labia – a memorable sight.' Gradually, he became less of a spectator. Each year he knew more people, went to grander, smarter parties, stayed in better houses. He lunched with Peggy Guggenheim on the terrace of her palazzo, which fascinated him with the extraordinary collection and its magical Grand Canal setting. He dined with the Duchess of Windsor, and stayed at the Palazzo Albrissi.

When I myself was 23 or so, I remember my parents' old friend, artist Teddy Millington-Drake looking at me and saying, 'Oh dear, you're not nearly as good-looking as your father was at your age… I can still see him today, walking across the Accademia Bridge in Venice. He was marvellous, so handsome, all dressed in white…' Teddy never worried too much about putting people at their ease, but the picture of my father, all in white, has stayed with me. I remember crossing the bridge with him myself, on one of

our last family holidays, a week in Venice just before my sister Edwina's wedding. We were going to the Accademia and stopped on the bridge, he pointing out every palazzo that he had stayed in each of those summers of the 1950s, each house where he had eaten and danced and slept.

By the time that he married, in 1960, my father was a sophisticated, habitual traveller. He knew the smarter cities of Europe and the USA well, and had friends in most of them. Even so, he always remained terribly English beneath it all, not so much unlike his austere Victorian father, with the national dread of foreign plumbing and kitchens. He would never really trust a foreigner, despite his many international friends. He loved Venetian food, but would really have been much happier eating it at Cecconi's in London than on the terrace at the Gritti, were it not for the view of Santa Maria della Salute. He was, however, hugely adventurous – for instance, going to Cuba for the first time just months before he died, terribly sick and weak, but determined to see it. It was not a success. In fact, he hated it and stayed only two nights, but he did go.

The Grander Tour

My mother, slightly dismayed to be photographed while having breakfast in bed at Villa Maser.

In the first years of their marriage, my parents did a great deal of travelling. Honeymooning in New York and the Bahamas gave way to long trips to Egypt, Africa and India, together with shorter visits in Europe. They went to visit all of my mother's many German cousins, staying in *Schloss* after *Schloss*, where my father drank in every detail of the old houses and the fading princely style of life within them. There were the Badens, whose home at Salem was so vast that the presence of a very large boarding school in one side was barely noticeable from the other, where the family still lived; and the Hohenlohes at Langenburg, where half the castle had been destroyed by fire just months before and was now being rebuilt exactly as it had been.

They went to Wolfsgarten, home of my grandfather's cousin, Ludwig Hessen, last prince of the Hesse-Darmstadt line from which his parents had come. This, the most atmospheric and fascinating of all these houses, is an old hunting lodge between Frankfurt and Darmstadt, the favourite country house of the last grand duke, Ernst Ludwig, an artistic soul who built the famous artists' colony at Darmstadt. Wolfsgarten is so stuffed with beautiful things and royal memorabilia (Ernst Ludwig's mother was Queen Victoria's daughter, Alice; his sister, Alix, was the last tsarina of Russia) that my father was hopelessly seduced by the place. Its rooms are a catalogue of historical styles, everything from the seventeenth century to the local

Jugendstil (or Art Nouveau). There is a famous Dürer hanging above the television, there are vitrines bursting with Fabergé, and albums of Princess Alice's watercolours with fawning notes by her painting tutor, John Ruskin.

Having seen most of England's great houses as a member of the Georgian Group, my father now went to stay in them, invited with my mother to summerhouse parties and winter shooting weekends. Everywhere he took with him his big Rolleiflex camera, filling album after album with large, hand-printed pictures of inspirational details of the houses. He saw everything – every tiny detail. He was fascinated by the way that dukes lived in their houses, not just by what they contained. It was the way that breakfast was served, the way the dogs were fed, the flowers and gold boxes and writing paper – all of the trappings of a vanishing way of life that had centuries of tradition and beauty wrapped up in them.

Every trip was made into a huge album of these photographs, the book specially made and covered in some particularly apt cloth or paper (usually bought on the trip). The albums have a casual, thrown-together style belying their great size and expense, with his one-word captions written big and rough in red crayon, masterpieces of understatement. They are quite different from his main scrapbooks, which are crammed with press cuttings, souvenirs, postcards, notes, each page carefully composed and styled, each moment preserved for posterity. The albums, instead, have a relaxed and effortless elegance about them. Many of the details pictured – whether an upholstery fabric or a roof-tile pattern, a wooden fretwork balustrade or an old painted sign – appear somewhere in his work, often years later.

This was certainly the Grander Tour. They went to Ethiopia, where they visited Emperor Haile Selassie, the Lion of Judah, King of Kings. My father photographed the leopards, chained up, lounging on the palace steps, and the emperor's car, which was sent to meet them. As they drove through Addis Ababa in the imperial Chevrolet, they were amazed to see the peasants on the roadside abase themselves in the dirt as the car swept past. Their audience with the emperor was a little awkward: they had prepared themselves to speak French throughout, told that he usually did this with English visitors, and of course spoke English with the French. Instead they were questioned at length in English about what they had been doing since their wedding and why, if they had really wanted to visit him, it had taken them several years to do so.

One stormy night, when they were camped on a mountaintop, my father went out of their tent 'to check the ropes', only to find a huge Nubian servant holding each of the tent pegs firmly in the ground. His first visit to India, where my mother had lived with her parents, was inevitably the most overwhelming of all these journeys. They happened to be in Delhi in March 1962, at the same moment as Jackie Kennedy and her sister, Lee Radziwill, and so moved from Prime Minister Nehru's house (where they had stayed initially) to make room for the American ladies, going to stay with the President at the old Lutyens Viceroy's House in which my mother had lived aged 17. My father's excitement at seeing the great sandstone pile – which was surely the most beautiful house of the twentieth century – was intense, and he went all over it, photographing details of everything, even the smallest bathroom. He revelled in the grandeur of the place, and was especially amused by the sign in their bedroom that advised guests that it took around fifteen minutes to walk to the dining room.

He was asked by Nehru to make a report on the state of Indian handicrafts and design, and began rather seriously, studying carefully what was then being made, making suggestions for what could be improved. Dhurries, Indian cotton rugs, at the time were all in late Victorian

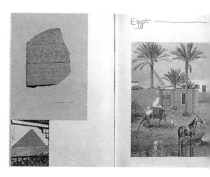

A typical travel scrapbook spread: two photographs, a print of the Rosetta Stone, and a single word – 'Egypt'.

A very relaxed leopard chained to the steps of Emperor Haile Selassie's palace, Addis Ababa, 1964.

My mother with Jawaharlal Nehru, all smiles at his house in Delhi, his customary rose in his buttonhole, 1962.

Objects arranged with characteristic precision on Winnie Portarlington's writing table, Earlywood, Ascot, 1962.

Hicks photographing Haile Selassie's Imperial Horse at their mud-walled stables, Ethiopia, 1964.

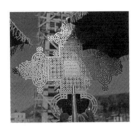

A young Coptic priest carrying a gold cross in Ethiopia, its Celtic spiral design later inspiring a Hicks carpet.

A tablescape: the collaged design for 'Chevron', based on pierced stone motifs seen in India, with a Chinese Pu-Tai.

My father's first geometric carpet, 'Y', inspired by turquoise mosaics seen on the Great Mosque at Isfahan.

colourways of brown, madder and ochre, heavy and depressing. Working with the beautiful Maharani of Jaipur, who had set up a factory to weave them, my father came up with new, fresh colours for the rugs in the now-familiar pastels and brighter pinks and turquoises.

Travel and Other Influences

Ever since his first trip to Provence aged 17, my father had loved to shop while travelling. That first purchase of *Directoire* engravings led on to more and better things. He would buy, voraciously, exotic local fabrics: silks in Benares; homespun striped stuff in Africa, Berber rugs in Morocco; a wooden bust of Louis XIV in France; endless baskets in Provence. At the time there were almost no shops selling exotic foreign things in London, and foreign things were still by definition exotic, in those long-lost days before our global economy. As well as buying, my parents were given wonderful Kente cloths by African visitors, a beautiful Tapa painted barkcloth by the Queen of Tonga and, of course, swathes of Indian stuffs of every description.

My father was also an inveterate collector of fragments of buildings and pretty bits of coral and shells. Just as he had pinched that old stone head from the ruin of Coggeshall church after the bomb hit it, he and I used to go together to falling-down houses in Bahamian villages near our house, and rescue old fretwork balusters and brackets. He would mount these architectural scavengings directly on to the wall in the Bahamas, or on to big boards back in England, together with other fragments, of English or Irish houses, of jobs that he had worked on. It was a modern version of the back corridor of Sir John Soane's museum, which is crowded with relics of old London, fast disappearing in Soane's 1820s.

All of this exotica became an important part of his decorating, and a great influence, too. His tablescapes got much of their energy and interest from mixing poor and rich objects, and many of the poor ones were collected abroad. More importantly, though, these travels gave him inspiration either directly or indirectly. Directly, he would see those exquisite, sophisticated Indian rooms whose walls are divided into well-proportioned panels by sharp, coloured borders cut into their polished plaster surface, and would imitate this technique back in London, Paris or New York using bands of cut paper or fabric webbing.

More indirectly, he created dozens of geometric carpet and fabric designs, many of the patterns taken from his immaculate and treasured 1854 copy of Owen Jones's *Grammar of Ornament*, but first seen by him in full effect on monuments in Persia (now Iran) and India, where such patterns are everywhere: in carved wood, glazed tiles, inlaid marble and pierced sandstone. The first of his famous carpets, the 'Y' design, was adapted from turquoise tiles that he photographed on the Great Mosque in Isfahan. He saw, he adapted and then used whatever interested him. In the same way, he would find good patterns in a saint's painted robes in a Byzantine icon, or in the marble floor of an old pharmacy.

My father was always looking, looking, looking. He was unable to see a seventeenth-century still-life without thinking how good the silver looked against the stitching of the Turkish carpet draped over the table. He had little interest in the brushwork, the symbolism, or any other quality that would appeal to art historians and connoisseurs. He was frequently more interested by the accessories, the details, the costumes, fabrics and furniture, than by the lines of the figures or the expressiveness of their faces, whether in Renaissance altarpieces or Ingres portraits. It was clues to the look of a life that he was searching for; details of atmosphere, and useful ideas for new designs of his own.

My father was never, as long as I knew him, without his little notepad, a black leather wallet with his 'H' logo on the back and gilt corners that held a single card, on which he would scribble notes and sketch details, usually on top of his appointments for the day typed out by his secretary. If this notepad was full up, he would use whatever else came to hand. We have files stuffed with the strange ephemera of his working life – napkins, tickets, itineraries, meeting agendas, all which contain sketches, ideas, solutions to design problems, or simply doodles, and all carefully preserved, just in case they would be required at a later date.

He saw architecural details everywhere: the giant Tuscan columns of Ledoux's saltworks, France, 1967.

Travelling with Mr Hicks

As is witnessed by my letters from my father, he travelled unceasingly. In those early years of exotic tourism, it was for pleasure, but as time passed it was more and more for work. He never tired of flying huge distances to look at beautiful things, however, and would combine the two so that his annual visit to Japan to see the twenty Japanese companies who still today make products with his name would be combined with visits to South Africa and Australia, both of which he loved. He liked nothing more than Colonial architecture, whether British government houses in Calcutta or Singapore, or vast Portuguese cathedrals in Goa or Brazil. South Africa and Australia were great favourites because of his many friends in both countries, and he never tired of his annual visits.

After my parents had made a couple of trips with my grandfather, the Hicks style of travelling became increasingly splendid. I distantly remember our arrivals at Nice airport in the summer, where the airport manager was persuaded to take us personally from the plane to our car. The car itself was a white Ford Mustang with electric roof, driven down from London by the chauffeur. We all had special luggage labels printed with our monograms and our names – orange on turquoise for the girls and my mother, turquoise on orange for my father and me.

Travels with my grandfather were not to be missed. In 1966, my parents went with him on an official visit – as Chief of the Defence Staff, head of the British armed forces – to West Africa. My father made a very amusing

album of the trip full of pictures of my grandfather, who loved to dress up, alternating between full naval regalia and bizarre local robes. Together with my uncle and aunt, they made an extraordinary trip to China in January 1970, while most of the country was completely closed. I got long and excited letters from the Great Wall, where my father was wrapped up warm in a coat of shiny tan leather with a lining of ocelot, made specially for the visit. Every dose of Mountbatten grandeur would result in renewed extravagance from his son-in-law.

For my father, who grew up (like many of his generation) fascinated by flight but not going on an aeroplane until his early twenties, flying was always an excitement. He loved to travel, he loved to fly. He would complain about every moment of the journey when he was older, but he still loved it. Up there in the clouds, with a drink and some solitude, he had time to write letters, to sketch and plan – and, above all, he was going somewhere. It was an unlikely place for him to be happy, stuck in an uncomfortable seat, in an unattractive interior, surrounded by 'ghastly' people he did not know, but happy he was.

He hated to fly with check-in luggage. For the last twenty years, he would only travel with one tiny carry-on bag, with a couple of fresh shirts and a book, either a Nancy Mitford or James Morris's *Pax Britannica*. With this and his trusty attaché case, a briefcase small enough to fit under the seat, light enough that he could write and sketch with it balanced on his knees, he was ready for anything.

A spiral cut into white marble in the Summer Palace, Peking; Hicks in China with his father-in-law, 1970.

My father's luggage label, turquoise and orange, with his name (always 'Mr David Hicks') and his 'H' logo.

My father, mother and I visiting the Acropolis, Athens, on a hot afternoon in September 1972.

David Hicks, London

In 1954, after his house at 22 South Eaton Place had been published in *House & Garden* and he had made a few successful small orders – a cushion here, a pair of curtains there – my father's career was beginning in earnest. He was determined to make a real impact from the start, and was obsessive about details. He had, for instance, little embroidered labels (made like fashion labels), saying, 'David Hicks, London', which were sewn on to every pair of curtains, every cushion. Making the transition to serious decorating work was slow, however.

A typical early job was the work he did for Sir Robert Adeane, a succesful banker who had bought an enormous house near Cambridge, which needed to be entirely redecorated. So my father would go down, very excited, with a hatbox full of materials. Lady Adeane would say, 'How nice to see you, dear boy. Now, let's go out in the garden and find some onions for lunch.' They would spend an hour in the vegetable garden, and then go back to the house, where they would sit down and have a gin and tonic. After lunch, Lady Adeane would say, 'I think it's time for a walk: let's go down to the end of the lake and see what's happened there.'

After several hours of this, my father, feeling slightly anxious, would say, 'You know, Lady Adeane, I'm sorry but I'm desperate that we haven't done any work at all. Sir Robert is going to be very cross if I tell him we haven't made any decisions.' 'Oh well, all right,' she would say. 'What d'you think, then?' And so they would decide something for the dining room, perhaps, but nothing else – at a rate of one room a week. It was a good, big job, though, and of course it was great publicity. My father then went into partnership with Tom Parr, with whom he opened a shop, Hicks and Parr – the antiques found by Parr, and the decorating by Hicks.

The two of them got more and more work from the American Mrs Gilbert Miller, for her big house on Hill Street in Mayfair and then for her Sussex country house. They would go down there every three weeks to do yet another room ready for her return the next summer. (She only came for the summer.) Tom was the perfect partner, having a lot of business sense, and did all the estimating. 'I was the creative one, really,' my father assured me. The partners worked behind a curtain under the stairs while doing estimates. In 1958, they then bought another shop about three doors away in the same building. Hicks would sit in one shop, with Parr in the other.

They both had vans with smartly painted 'Hicks and Parr' name-boards that they could take out in order to drive through the Royal Parks, which to this day do not allow trade vehicles. They were big shooting brakes – estate cars – with long windows in the back, to which they had metal housings fitted so they could drop the name-boards in. The pair would always drive around together, in convoy, in order to look as though they had a lot of work. Driving through smart streets on very hot days, they would also keep the windows tight shut so that people would think they had air conditioning. The moment they crossed Sloane Square and got to the King's Road, however, they let the windows down, knowing that no potential clients lived in Chelsea. 'At traffic lights,' he told me, 'we used to relish people's amazed looks. We were both up to a lot of stylish tricks.'

The partnership ended when my father married in 1960, setting up on his own as David Hicks Limited. Tom Parr took a share of the respectable old firm of Colefax & Fowler, which he quietly built over the next twenty years into the great institution it is today. They remained firm friends, although their different views on life became gradually more marked. As my father recalled, 'Tom was always very anti-publicity, which I thought was very odd. He has always rather shunned publicity, while I've always rather encouraged it.'

Meeting the Mountbattens

My father met my mother, Pamela Mountbatten, in 1959 and he, impulsive as ever, asked her almost immediately how many children she wanted to have when they were married. He was utterly relentless and swept her off her feet. For the first part of their courtship, my father (who had been fascinated by the Mountbattens for years) thought that perhaps they were, as he put it, 'estranged' from their younger daughter, since she never mentioned them. My mother, of course, was merely concerned that her rather intimidating parents would frighten away this charming young man.

After a few weeks, she finally asked him to meet them, at a military review where my grandfather was taking the salute. My father had first become aware of the Mountbattens when my grandfather was Viceroy. Young David, in his Essex village, had seen a picture of the new Viceroy and Vicereine in Delhi, beside their thrones. 'I was so badly educated', he told me, 'that I didn't really know what a Viceroy was, but I do remember thinking they were a stunning-looking couple, and frightfully grand.'

When he finally did meet them, my father went in black tie to their house in Wilton Crescent. There were already two motorcycle police outside, and Lord Mountbatten's car with his flag on it. Collier (their 'very grand butler') showed him into the library, where my grandmother Edwina Mountbatten was standing, looking 'absolutely marvellous in evening dress, the most charismatic woman I've ever set eyes on. Really wonderful looking. You didn't notice the fact that her hair was a bit auburn. I was bowled over by her.' My mother was being

very quiet indeed, of course, and letting her mother do all the talking – which she did, saying she knew all about my father's work, what he had done for the Bessboroughs and the Fairbankses, and how clever he must be.

There was then the most tremendous noise on the staircase and Lord Mountbatten came crashing down in full evening dress, in black tie but naval style, a 'monkey jacket' with lots of gold braid and, of course, all his medals and the Order of the Garter and everything ('Overwhelming, like a sort of avalanche arriving'). My mother said, 'Hello, Daddy, this is David Hicks.' 'Evening,' he barked. 'Now, let's go, we've got two and a half minutes to be in the car…' They got in the car and he started shouting at his Royal Marines driver, 'Now, Sergeant Riley, I don't want to arrive early. We've got twenty-eight minutes to get there in.' 'Yes, sir, but we've got outriders…' 'I don't care if we have outriders. Get there exactly on time. We'd better go round the block, must get there absolutely on time.'

My father remembered this as 'the most amazing performance'. My mother and he were sitting on the jump seats, so 'I got the full blast of this shouting through the partition. But it was lovely and glamorous, whizzing through all the red traffic lights.' They arrived at Olympia, where a small crowd had gathered, all shouting for Mountbatten. Afterwards they went back to supper at the house on Wilton Crescent – which was absolutely delicious – in the dining room, which had a big alcove either side of the fireplace, 'stuffed with unbelievable silver', a Joshua Reynolds portrait over the chimney, and a set of very rare, early eighteenth-century red lacquer chairs, on which they sat.

My father, of course, took everything in. As well as the butler, there was a naval steward in a blue battledress uniform, loosely modelled on the wartime royal footman's livery but with a large, embroidered Mountbatten cypher on the pocket in place of the king's. The conversation was

My father with his pug, Algy, around the time that he met my mother, 1959.

My parents' engagement photograph, 1959.

My grandparents in front of their viceregal thrones in the Durbar Hall, on arrival in New Delhi, 1947.

My parents, marrying in a snowstorm, Romsey Abbey, Hampshire, 13 January 1960.

A typical early, outspoken newspaper interview with England's most famous interior decorator, 1961.

Prodding the ceiling, watched by Helena Rubenstein, in her new London apartment, then in process, 1961.

mostly about what they were doing the next day or the next weekend. My grandfather barely spoke to my father (what could he have found to talk about to this nervous young interior decorator?), but my grandmother made up for this by chatting away to him and making him feel clever, talented and important. She smoked between courses and drank whisky throughout dinner, which he thought very sophisticated and, of course, it meant that *he* could too.

Starting Afresh

After a wildly glamorous, fairytale wedding (which took place in drifting snow in January 1960), a lengthy honeymoon, my grandmother's death and the purchase of Britwell – all of which happened in a blaze of publicity – my father had to start more or less all over again. His career had been marvellous until then, with client after client, aristocracy and upstart hairdressers alike. Now he suddenly found himself without a job. Everyone he knew simply assumed that he would no longer work at all, but would become an escort to my mother, going from royal house to friend's yacht, by her side as she performed her various charitable duties.

He was desperate. To counter the wrong impression everyone had formed, and taking advantage of his new-found celebrity as the Mountbatten son-in-law, he gave newspaper interviews with his outspoken and forthright views on decoration and taste; redesigned council flats for free for magazines; and started to work as a design consultant for various manufacturers who welcomed this high-profile young man. Eventually jobs did start to come in. One of the best was beauty doyenne Helena Rubenstein, whose new apartment overlooking Hyde Park needed a high-profile makeover – and who better than young David Hicks?

This early commission was hugely important to his career, partly because of the prestige it won him, and the tremendous publicity in the fashion magazines that were to promote this interior designer as much (or more than) the interiors' journals – for the first few years, at least. In addition to this, however, Madame Rubenstein's masterly command of her world and her unerring, timeless grasp of style were very influential on his rapidly forming way of working. She had used every decorator of interest, creating a succession of famous houses in New York and Paris. He had the good sense to let her lead, accommodating a bizarre collection of disparate elements, including heavy Victorian Belter furniture and African masks in an ugly, low-ceilinged space.

At the very first meeting in the apartment, where builders were already at work removing old partition walls, he and Madame sat on an old trunk in a corner. He asked her what she had thought of as a colour for the walls. She called for her assistant to bring some scissors and reached down to the hem of her Balenciaga dress, cutting a piece of its purple silk and handing it to my father, who proceeded to have a rough woollen 'tweed' dyed to that precise shade and hung on the walls. Even while the job was in the making, a colour sketch of the finished drawing room was published. When complete, every corner was photographed, so much so that it occupies pages and pages of his scrapbook for 1961.

After a couple of years, he closed the shop he had kept on from Hicks and Parr, setting up instead a small office in the basement of his new house in St Leonard's Terrace, near Sloane Square. The office remained here for several years, and I remember it well from London visits as a child, when we would sneak in to see what was going on. The glazed doors to the garden were screened with pierced Moroccan wooden shutters, whose geometric quality reflected some of the small-scale geometric patterns that were starting to emerge from the office. Assistants were recruited to draw up designs found in old sources like *The Grammar of Ornament*, painting different colourways in gouache for DH's approval or rejection.

The patterns were then starting to turn into carpets (first woven for his bathroom and library at Britwell in 1961) and fabrics (first printed for my parents' London bedroom in 1963). Early sample boards from jobs of this time show how many of his own designs were used in each job, or rather how few of others'. Colour was hugely important to him. I found one sample of a searing, eye-jarringly bright-green 'tweed' with a label attached from the dyers' lab: 'Cannot be achieved any brighter'. He always described the kind of rough, open-weave wool or cotton that he loved to use in strong, plain colours as 'tweed', much to the confusion of his imitators, who, reading this term in his books, would rush off to a furnishing fabric showroom, only to be sent on to a tailor's supplier.

The Interior Decorator

The instant celebrity that had accompanied his marrying the Mountbattens' daughter may have put off some potential clients, but it certainly made my father the highest-profile decorator of the day, and the first to become known to the general public and to make a name for himself in the wider world beyond the drawing rooms of Belgravia. My grandfather had always been a master of self-promotion, from his honeymoon in Hollywood in 1922, when Charlie Chaplin made a home movie with the glamorous newlyweds, onwards through his entire glittering, very public career, until the late 1960s, when he made not one television programme about his life but an entire series – twelve programmes covering the full range of *The Life and Times of Lord Mountbatten*.

My father longed to achieve a fraction of this fame and hungrily pursued every bit of press coverage that he could find. Among these was a 1964 television documentary, *The Interior Decorator*, which cut from questioning 'members of the public' on the street about their feelings on decorating to film of my father in the office, at the upholsterer's and meeting with clients. The client they chose, Mrs S, had a house on St Leonard's Terrace, a few doors down from his own. He had decorated the drawing room the previous year, taking gold objects from the client's extraordinary collection and mounting them on little gold shelves floating against walls stretched with bottle-green silk velvet, in one of the most glamorous and luxurious interiors of all time.

'This first discussion', my father explained in a voiceover, 'in an empty room is the crucial one, as the design is nearly always finalized then.' The client explained that, with her beautiful but very formal drawing room downstairs, in this sitting room she was instead looking for an informal, relaxed look, centred on her collection of Nicolas de Staël paintings. They settled on an off-white scheme, to 'paint the walls just off-white, with a little bit of pink to warm it, because the room has a rather dull, northerly aspect'. They agreed on a provincial French stone fireplace, with my father focusing immediately on the finishing touches, and determined to 'avoid having the ordinary arrangement on the shelf of a clock and two candlesticks, instead have a simple treatment of big, bold flowers on one side and a piece of modern sculpture, maybe, on the other'.

The only disagreement was over what to do at the windows. My father suggested his new favourite treatment – cloth-covered shutters – but Mrs S was adamant: 'No, we've got shutters upstairs, and in the drawing room we've got this enclosed feeling, not another shut-in room.' And so a new idea immediately popped into his head, for

'Clinch' – a Hicks repeat design .

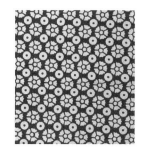

'Mint Flower' – what my father called a geo-floral.

In Keith Lichtenstein's apartment, my father arranged six ancient heads beneath three Francis Bacons in 1969.

Mrs S's Chelsea drawing room with walls of bottle-green silk velvet and her collection of pre-Columbian gold.

Mrs S's dining room, with a red Hicks carpet jostling for attention with the yellow Welsh blanket tablecloth.

Opposite: Hicks with pug dog; Hicks engaged; wedding invitation; emerging from the Abbey into the snow; sketches for Helena Rubinstein's bedroom, hall and living room – published in Queen magazine before it was finished – and a photograph of it complete.

it was ever one of his strictures that you must always, always appear to have instant solutions to any problem: 'If you won't have shutters…then we could have very, very simple curtains with a simple heading at the top, in rough, rather inexpensive material, rather knobbly in texture and running an upholsterer's braid down the leading edge.' Mrs S was delighted. 'Much better. Thank you, David.'

The finished house was photographed many times, and was such a success that my father told me he found it still untouched, still glamorous as ever, thirty years later. The television documentary probably did nothing to help his career, beyond getting ever more press exposure. He thrilled to each new article, each new mention. He redecorated a tiny two-bedroom Nottingham council flat, sponsored by a national newspaper, which recorded every moment, from his first arrival in his long, strawberry-bronze-coloured Cadillac. In response to this, satirical magazine *Private Eye* ran a spoof article on 'David Slick', poking around a derelict hovel in which a filthy homeless woman was squatting, with 'Slick' throwing his arms in the air with delight, exclaiming, 'I wouldn't touch a thing! It's perfect! The glamour of it all!' My father, of course, was thrilled, deeply flattered by the attention, whatever they actually said about him.

Vidal Sassoon, whose first flat had the David Hicks treatment in 1958, told me a story of my father being begged and implored by a certain client to get her a Francis Bacon painting, since he knew the artist quite well. According to Vidal's story, my father went to the woman's house to hang the picture, but found her looking at it upside down. Furious at this sign of total philistinism, he tore the picture from the hands of his protesting client and took it straight back to Bacon. Whether true or not, the reputation that he was achieving with such movers and shakers of the era as Vidal – the first, original and greatest of the star hairdressers – was obviously very important.

Charm Never Hurts

About his early success, my father said, 'It is a difficult thing to say, but I think charm never hurts.' This is doubtless true, but he was also tremendously gifted and had an unerring sense of what someone would or would not respond to, and of how to handle the most reluctant, obstinate or timid client so that they would, in the end, find themselves with the kind of interior that he could proudly call his own and want to publish in magazines and his books. Over years of working, in the early days sharing and learning tricks of the trade with other designers, he developed a legion of clever techniques that made all this possible.

One of his assistants – who had gone on to work for a succession of unpleasant, selfish and egotistical designers who never once passed on so much as a hint of their methods – told me that he had given her the best possible clue while in a taxi returning from meeting a client in her new house. How, the assistant had asked, could he have guessed so surely that the lady would like that curious apricot colour he had suggested for her bedroom? 'Ah,' he replied sagely. 'You didn't notice the colour of her dress? A lady always likes her walls the same colour as her clothes.' Whether he first learned this from Madame Rubenstein, from John Fowler (for whom he worked for about a week), from his friend Billy Baldwin, or just from intuition, I will never know, but it was one of his maxims.

Charm never does hurt, especially when combined with a huge talent, a great sense of humour and utmost professionalism. My father's temperament was completely that of an artist – moody, irascible, excitable and prone to throwing tantrums. Rarely, however, did he allow this to get in the way of his work. He might storm out of a meeting one day, but he was not proud, and the next day would see him back on form, wooing and charming his clients into support of whatever compromise he could find in his design scheme that would keep everyone happy.

Admiral of the Fleet
Earl & Countess Mountbatten of Burma
request the pleasure of your company
at the Wedding of their daughter
Pamela
with
Mr. David Hicks
at Romsey Abbey at 3.0 p.m.
and afterwards at Broadlands
on Wednesday, 13th January 1960

Madame's bedroom
looking from hall door towards
window which is flanked by
vitrines full of Opalines.

Entrance Hall: seen from left.
Faux Black granite walls : White rustication & ceiling
Black & white vinyl floor
Bank furniture including 2 scarlet cushioned Buhle stools

Belgravia
3771

...KS LIMITED

Rubenstein flat preview sketch in 'Queen'

BRITWELL | 39

1. THE WEDDING OF LADY PAMELA MOUNTBATTEN AND MR. DAVID HICKS

The couple left Romsey Abbey in a snowstorm

Two weddings, one in Paris, the other in Hampshire,
have each excited a nation with their demonstration of

Marrying in the grand manner

Flying Between New York and Nassau, 1967 ....

My most darling Pammy

It has been exciting — almost daily I've been in a newspaper but also of course pretty hectic. I dined with Ethel Merman, I'm in American Vogue. I dined with Peggy Bernier and Philip Johnson's coming to drinks with Senator Javits on the 14th — I dine with Charlotte Niarchos Ford on the 13th and etc. I dined with Raymond Loewy — I'm on the cover of Home Furnishings Daily *in the longest interview ever printed! I'm to design fabrics for release in January for Connaissance. Amanda Burden's stairs are covered in Hicks carpet. I'm on the cover of* L'Oeil *and Mrs Robert E. Scull wants me on the 15th! (very good pop pictures). Bloomingdale's have never paid anyone for doing room-settings before and look as though they may now! I sold 18 books in Philadelphia and 200 yards of carpet.*

A man presented me last night with a gouache of the Britwell drawing room — he came with his editor from Interior Design *magazine. Yesterday (my 8th day) I had 4 interviews! Everybody wants to own me and help. Vogue & Peggy Bernier are very sweetly thrilled by my success. When do I make some money? I need a business manager. I have press cuttings the like of which you've never seen! I've literally had no time to clean my teeth because each night there's been a dinner in my honour, each day a lunch with important Editors in wonderful restaurants and in between interviews I've occasionally had a minute to go to the carpet showroom where there are always 15 people who have waited 2 or 3 hours to meet me!*

We did have 476 decorators at the opening! I spent 2 hours gossiping with Billy Baldwin on Sunday morning. He's off to Madrid today to work there.

Bloomingdale's may take the objects, pottery, costume jewellery, men's clothes, fabrics, carpets, tables, posters etc. My darling you would have hated it all but it would have been fun to have met you tomorrow and recounted it all. I'll call you when I get in this afternoon from Nassau. Now we are over the Caribbean and it's so blue & beautiful — I do wish you were here. Please give the children my love — I only hope I can remember what they wanted — it was a new Dolly & raincoat wasn't it & an American Bulldozer or Lorry?

I think in the end I was given a toy VW Beetle — big and white, with blue headlamps that worked — which trundled around the nursery at Britwell. We had a big map of the world on the wall and would search with my mother, or with the nanny if they were both away, for where on the map my father had got to on his travels. According to his own map, he was clearly headed very much in the right direction, as the excitement of this letter to my mother shows. He was nonstop in those days, and New York was a second home, especially once he had struck a deal with the St Regis Hotel to decorate a David Hicks Suite for them (which would be kept at his disposal whenever he was in the city).

America: An Inspiration

My father first went to America in 1956. He was 27 years old and had been nowhere more distant than Italy or France. His excitement at seeing America for the first time was tremendous. From childhood, like everyone, he had been fascinated by America and thought Americans were very glamorous, with their 'movie accents'. In the War, they had an American woman soldier billeted on them with 'wonderful legs, marvellous stockings, very good ankles', whom young David thought very glamorous. Finally reaching the United States was a great thrill for him.

In England at the time, there was hardly such a thing as a professional interior decorator or designer. Both architects and furniture designers were seen as professionals, and then there were antique- or decorating-shop owners, but actual professional decorators were scarcely acknowledged. There were a few exceptions, like John Fowler and Felix Harbord, but they tended to be seen as gentleman amateurs who helped their friends with their houses, rather like the gentleman amateur architects of the eighteenth century. My father, starting his career three years before, was afraid he might be 'branded for life with the suede shoes, mauve tie image which I loathed'.

Arriving in New York, he discovered that decorators were seen as proper professionals, just like architects, which was a revelation to him. Where England was still mired in the hangover of Victoriana, and to be 'in trade' was still something of a stigma, here he found himself taken seriously. This was hugely important in his professional development, and he took back to England with him a new-found confidence and seriousness that was to help transform the profession in the UK. It was a liberating and energizing feeling, to be young, talented and English, free from the oppressive old-world culture of London, in the most modern, sophisticated country in the world, whose economic boom was still going strong, where everything was new and gleaming, where nothing seemed impossible.

Mies van der Rohe's Seagram building was then in construction, the very definition of modernity. Every time I saw my father in New York, whenever we passed the building on Park Avenue he would describe to me the excitement he had felt on first seeing it going up, back in 1956. From New York, he went out to the West Coast, where he stayed with Tony Hail, then a young San Franciscan decorator and, like him, just starting out. Tony

showed him California and the new local style of decorating – that easy, relaxed look of subtle beige and off-white, mixing antiques and modern furniture and pictures. Tony sent him to Santa Barbara to see Wright Luddington, whose modern house and collection my father always rated as one of the most exciting and beautiful he had ever seen.

Returning to London, equipped with a new outlook and a new ambition, both essentially American, my father set about his career in earnest. Early clients from this time have told me how Hicks and Parr was the only decorating firm in London to give proper estimates and to work in a serious, professional way. At the time decorators were seen not only as unprofessional but also as getting up to the sort of tricks for which Syrie Maugham had been famous, with vagaries of restoration and invoicing being rife. That their firm was not like this is due in part to Tom Parr's years working at the General Trading Company (an influential and stylish shop still in its Sloane Street quarters today), but also, I am sure, partly due to my father's American visit.

He returned to the States every year thereafter. In 1960 my parents began their honeymoon on the *Queen Mary*, spending their wedding night in Southampton harbour as the only passengers on the vast ship, with the crew of hundreds attending to their every need. The other passengers joined the ship the next day, and they sailed for New York. Bad weather delayed them, but the newlyweds were photographed on arrival, their picture appearing on the front of the *Post* under the heading 'Just a couple of Hicks!' A day late, they missed a large cocktail party that had been given for them. Undeterred, their host persuaded most of his guests to return the following night to finally meet the young honeymooners.

My mother had lived in New York for a year as a girl, sent there with her sister as refugees from the London

Riding a wave of geometric carpet to success in the United States, 1967.

My father photographed in Wright Luddington's living room, Santa Barbara, and a lunch party in California, first American trip, 1956.

On a breakfast TV chat show with the hostess and David Hicks on Bathrooms, somewhere in America, 1970.

Being interviewed with my mother, during their US tour to promote the Hicks sheets for J. P. Stevens, 1969.

On the Stevens company jet, flying from one city to another, 1970.

Blitz by my grandmother, who worried that her Jewish blood would mean their certain death if a Nazi invasion of England succeeded. They had lived in oppressive splendour with Mrs Cornelius Vanderbilt at her enormous mansion on Fifth Avenue, now the Neue Galerie. In 1960, my parents paid visits all over the city, to everyone from my mother's old family friends to celebrities such as Greta Garbo, who told my mother, 'With your eyes and his profile, my dear, you will have the most beautiful children.'

Visiting Johnson

One day they went to lunch with architect Philip Johnson, whom my father had met on previous visits. They took the elevator up to his office, then on one of the higher floors of the Seagram building, which he had built in collaboration with Mies van der Rohe. They emerged into a vast, long space crowded with desks, at which numberless architects were hunched over plans, and were led through the space to Johnson's office at the far end, a large, quite empty room with two walls of glass looking downtown along Park Avenue. They sat and chatted for a while, my father fascinated by the completely empty desk that held only a stack of plain white paper and a handsome, modern pot holding fifty perfectly sharp, identical pencils.

After a while, the door opened and an assistant appeared carrying two apparently identical samples of white marble. Without a word, Johnson tapped one of them and the assistant left. My father was hugely impressed by this performance, which suggested that the marble was to clad some vast new building, while the similarity of the samples clearly demanded a rare precision of eye. They then went downstairs to the Four Seasons Hotel and ate with Johnson at his regular table. Twenty-one years later, I was given lunch by another of my father's friends, Rosamond Bernier, and taken over to Johnson's

table, where he still sat. I was fascinated by his perfectly domed head and his perfectly circular glasses. The sense of theatre that surrounded Johnson, not unlike that around my grandfather, appealed strongly to my father.

Allegra and I lived in New York (for the first two years of our marriage), and one day went with my father out to New Canaan, where Johnson and his friend David Whitney gave us tea in the famous Glass House that he had built forty years before. The two old men competed for how many of their old friends were now dead, each thrilled to surprise the other with news of another one's passing. Johnson was a true showman, nimbly darting from one part of his demesne to another, taking us into the strange underground gallery, where he flicked through his amazing collection of huge canvases by Warhol, Rosenquist, Stella, Johns, all mounted on three rotating arms that spun like overscaled fans.

On that cold winter afternoon, we ended the tour in the Glass House, which had been restored a few years before and was immaculate. What a vision, what a style – the perfect Mies furniture, the walls of glass, the single piece of art, a Claude landscape on a stainless-steel easel. The free-standing kitchen, which had all of its original 1947 equipment, seemed never to have been used, and it took our hosts a good thirty minutes to locate a brand-new-looking 1947 kettle, teapot and cups for the tea they had brought over from the clapboard house on the edge of the property where they actually lived. My father was greatly amused by this performance, and he teased Johnson about the kitchen for the rest of the visit. We drove back into the city, my father reminiscing like mad.

My father hired a young assistant in London around 1963, an American named Mark Hampton who worked in the little office in our basement for three years before he married and moved back to New York, initially as the David Hicks Associate. Many of the early, gouache carpet designs and fabric colourways have Mark's already-distinctive, elegant italic handwriting on the back, so he must have spent a lot of the time with a brush in his hand. Mark, of course, became one of America's greatest decorators (among his better commissions was work at the White House for the first President Bush). When they arrived in New York, Mark and Duane's first married home was a small apartment on 66th Street with an all-black-and-white living room, designed by my father as a wedding present to his ex-assistant.

This first room was entirely my father – hard, graphic and frighteningly stylish. The Hamptons moved house twice in rapid succession, and each new apartment had elements from the old, gradually mixed with new pieces. The first thing to go was the lack of colour, and Mark went for the red walls of which he never tired. The publication of the first book, *David Hicks on Decorating* (1966), brought him suddenly to the attention of the New York market, with a snowballing succession of clients and jobs, all handled initially by Mark Hampton with the help of architect Theodore Triant. The early days were great fun, and the excitement of his letters to my mother show clearly how excited he was about his new work.

Working in New York

My father worked for clients in New York from 1966 to about 1973. At one point he was busy on several different apartments at the same time, and would walk down Fifth Avenue from one to another, joking that he would remove the *parquet de Versailles* from one, only to have it installed in the other. Where he found parquet, he insisted the only thing was carpet. Where he found carpet, only wood would do. Pine panelling was removed, for one of his geometric printed fabrics to be stretched in its place, while painted wood in another apartment was stripped back to the original pine.

While London clients would keep him on a tight rein, allowing only so many of his ideas, insisting on keeping much of their old furniture and pictures, most of these new American jobs presented a clean slate. This designer, after all, had done both Helena Rubenstein's apartment and the Prince of Wales' first set of rooms. His imagination was allowed free rein and he would design every new piece of furniture, even small sculptures in Perspex that were the logical extension of the Perspex cases he was making to hold precious objects. If the clients had a badly framed Picasso, he would have it redone in stainless steel.

When one of these apartments was completed and about to be photographed, my father arranged some flowers on the chimneypiece. He was amazed to come back six months later and see exactly the same arrangement, the now-out-of-season flowers having been specially flown in, as though an essential part of his creation. Moving the vase to one side, he found its outline carefully drawn on the shelf, with a list of the flowers that he had originally placed there. A letter from designer Van Day Truex testifies to the effect that Hicks designs, and his books in particular, were having in America:

925 Park Avenue, New York 10028,
January 19th 1967
Dear David,
Your book is a delight – rewarding! It just records again what I feel about you – In general, no matter what project you undertake – from the remodelled little flat – the bathroom – the kitchen – to the 'stately halls' – there is clear style – and elegance – and precision. It's the direct approach – you don't quibble – you never get fussy – and what I admire is the result of what I call your 'z-ray' eye and observation – all that you glean from anything – anyone – and everywhere – and transform into your personal statement.

Presenting new Hicks fabrics with a model wearing his 'Zed' design as bikini and sunhat, Chicago, 1970.

Another early-morning TV appearance, with fabrics and David Hicks geometric monogram ties, 1970.

Mark and Duane Hampton's first, entirely black and white, New York apartment on 66th Street.

President Nixon in his newly redecorated bowling alley at the White House, with David Hicks wallpaper, 1971.

Showing the Apollo 14 astronauts my drawing of a spaceman, in the David Hicks Suite at the St Regis, 1971.

The American press just loved 'the Midas of Interior Design', with his outrageous fees.

So many have so little taste, because they're blind – thinking the Almighty handed it to them (I'm talking of most decorators and designers) – they turn out their puny efforts. If I have a little taste – (and I mean 'little') – it's because I haven't been too insensitive – I've wanted to acquire it – and I've been fortunate indeed to have come into contact with others possessing taste and flair – and each day my judgment is better – your book makes it better! Thank you!

In 1968 he was commissioned by J. P. Stevens, the American textile giant, to design sheets and towels for them, and he spent several weeks of the next year touring the USA in the company jet, accompanied by my mother, doing a city a day, with TV interviews, lectures and showroom openings. As part of the promotion, the DH-designed Stevens sheeting was used to make new bed-hangings in all of our houses, even stuck on the walls of my bedroom and several bathrooms. Stevens made a wonderful promotional film with us children jumping into Stevens-sheeted beds and 'David Hicks, the designer of today', tanned and shirtless, glamorously racing his speedboat past washing lines of the sheets strung outside the little harbour at Fréjus.

One of the many Stevens-sheeted beds was the glamorous baldachin in the David Hicks Suite at the St Regis in New York. For as long as he was working in the city, this was home away from home. He adored living in a hotel, but in his own rooms, and loved the glamour of opening the door with its brass plaque reading 'The David Hicks Suite'.

One of the best Hicks New York stories was when one day Mark Hampton telephoned him, asking him when he was free to fly to New York for lunch with Mrs B, whom my father took to be a new client, and so asked what the job was. 'No job,' Mark explained. 'She just wants to meet you, is willing to pay a fee and fly you over, restaurant and guests of your choice. We could look at some jobs at the same time…'

My father flew over a week later, and had a marvellous lunch at Le Cirque with all his friends and Mrs B, who was perfectly nice and sat quietly between Hicks and Hampton. Towards the end of the meal, Tony Snowdon came in, walked over and chatted with my father, who introduced him to Mrs B. When he walked away, she turned to Mark, a little confused, and inquired who that was. 'That's Lord Snowdon,' Mark explained. 'You know, the photographer, the Queen of England's brother-in-law.' 'Oh, my God,' said Mrs B. 'Is that extra?'

The End of America

In 1972–3, a series of little annoyances occurred that put my father off working in New York and effectively ended his career in the USA. The first was checking into the St Regis to be told that Liza Minnelli was in 'his' suite and he would have to go in a normal room. He stormed out of the hotel and never stayed there again. Hicks geometric carpets, which had been a runaway success and so much part of his style, suddenly started to pop up in every showroom, with designs just different enough that it was impossible to sue for copyright infringement. Whatever he might say to clients about the quality of the ones he had woven for them, they could not avoid seeing what was basically the same thing suddenly appearing everywhere. Paperback writers might talk about a glamorous house having 'a real David Hicks carpet, not one of those cheap knock-offs from Third Avenue', but who could tell the difference in reality?

There followed a severe blow when his new book *David Hicks on Home Decoration* (or *Decoration – 5* in England) was sold by the US distributors to a remainder house and was suddenly all over town discounted to a

tenth of its retail price, along with the two previous books. The end of all this saw my father sitting morosely in a New York lawyer's office for days on end, locked in arbitration over the publishing contract. His company had already sued the main imitator of the carpets without success, and here they were with more legal costs, getting nowhere. In the end they bought up the stock of books, but not before utter disenchantment had set in.

Back in 1971, my father had written the following letter, to a potential associate designer in Boston. I think it gives a fascinating insight into his working methods, both with clients and with his associates:

Perhaps I might take this opportunity of explaining my philosophy about decoration – particularly in relation to the American client, as it will differ quite considerably, I expect, from your own. I always try to get them to commit themselves to the kind of atmosphere, the kind of style and decoration that they themselves are seeking. With apparent ease and subtlety I suggest various schemes which might suit the various rooms. The moment I see them bite I clamp down on the scheme as tight and as hard as I can and make remarks like 'Well, that is very good for the dining room. I think that we can feel that although it is not absolutely definite, we have got a scheme that we all like for that particular room. Now let us move on to the next room.'

In discussing the next room we reject, of course, any similarity in scheme or colour to the previous room and refer to the previous room's scheme as if it were a completely definite decision. In this way I guide them through the house, trying not to let them change their minds and always looking to simplify the situation – indecision and changes of mind are a nightmare to the professional interior designer. Clients' friends must

always be kept well out of the picture and, if possible, it is much easier to deal with one or other of the couple.

Naturally, in my position, time is my enemy and I therefore always appreciated tremendously the way Mark Hampton and also Fleur Vulliod, my associate in Switzerland, have listened patiently while I have done all the creative talking, merely making copious notes of every decision. They have always seen their job at this stage of the development of the work as being a silent, accurate, alert assistant.

When I am in London they become associates and minor details which may have been overlooked by me at the time can be filled in by them because they are people of taste whom I admire and know I can rely on as, indeed, I can on you. If you think there is some point which you feel is really desperately important, please contribute to the action, but otherwise try to let me have the stage completely. It is easier to discuss things when we are away from the client, and alternatives or additional ideas can be suggested at a later meeting.'

More images of Hicks touring the USA, 1970, promoting his sheet and towel collection for Stevens.

America had inspired him, had charged him with the drive to become a serious professional, to achieve the status in England that professional designers had in the USA. He found working in the States an adventure, but not without its drawbacks. I remember him telling me that at one stage he had made the conscious decision not to make his career in America, despite the certain success that he foresaw there, because he could not bear to live more there than in his beloved England, especially to be away so much from his beautiful Britwell. My mother would have hated it, and in the end the American adventure came to an end. He continued to visit often, of course – at least once a year – but no longer with the same involvement.

Roquebrune

One of the few houses that my father truly admired, and which influenced him enormously, was La Fiorentina on Cap Ferrat in the south of France. He described his first visit as 'the key to another whole world. A magic world. Wonderful food, fascinating people, a marvellous, grand house, mammoth swimming pool right on the sea.' Rory Cameron, whose mother Lady Kenmare had bought the house just before the War, lived there in the summer with huge amounts of style and taste, and the place was utter perfection. The house has a vast Palladian portico and a wonderful garden looking across to the Alpes Maritimes behind Monte Carlo.

Everything about La Fiorentina and the life lived in it was inspiring for my father, who was 25 when he first went there. Every summer thereafter he went to stay with Rory, who was a great friend and became godfather to my sister Edwina. The old visitors' book, in which guests were required to write a poem or draw a sketch as well as sign, had a pretty watercolour from each of these visits. When Rory sold the house and moved into the small guesthouse next door, Le Clos Fiorentina, Billy Baldwin decorated the big house for its new owners, using, ironically enough, a David Hicks geometric carpet in the dining room. A few years later, Rory sold this too, and my father decorated Le Clos for the new owners who, later still, sold on to Hubert de Givenchy.

In 1966, partly to console my father after his mother Iris's death, my parents bought an enchanting eighteenth-century house on the main square of a little village called Roquebrune-sur-Argens, about fifteen miles inland from Fréjus in the south of France. The village was a sleepy, peaceful little place, far from the hectic life of St Tropez just along the coast. The house was untouched, a simple but grand town house with a pretty, curving stair, a balcony looking on to the square, and a roofed terrace on top that looked behind to the church and the mountain of Roquebrune. My own room looked out this side, too, and I well remember the deafening crash of the church bells that would wake me in the morning.

The house had nothing in common with La Fiorentina, none of its grandeur of architecture or position – all of which were reflected instead in Britwell. The only similarities with Rory's house were the location in the south of France and an atmosphere of relaxed elegance. Unlike Britwell, this was a small holiday house, somewhere for summer holidays with us children, and relaxing breaks at other moments of the year; but most of all it was another house for my father to get his teeth into, another laboratory for his decorating ideas. I see parallels between this big house in a village and the Essex houses that he remembered from his own childhood and, indeed, the very first thing he did was to pack up most of Iris's dark, English country furniture and send it down to the new house in France.

These old pieces of furniture were all that my father had left from his own heritage. One piece he was particularly fond of, a tall dresser named (after some otherwise-forgotten housekeeper) 'Mrs Wilson'. Swamped by my mother's very much grander possessions and background, all of which he worshipped, he did need some presence of his own past in his life, and here it was. They were joined by a few carefully chosen pieces of my Mountbatten grandmother's, like four chairs made in 1937 for her apartment, at Brook House on Park Lane, in imitation of Empire-period Jacob swan chairs at Malmaison, an Empire ormolu incense burner and a huge chunk of petrified tree trunk, a curiosity that had stood in Sir Ernest Cassel's library at Brook House.

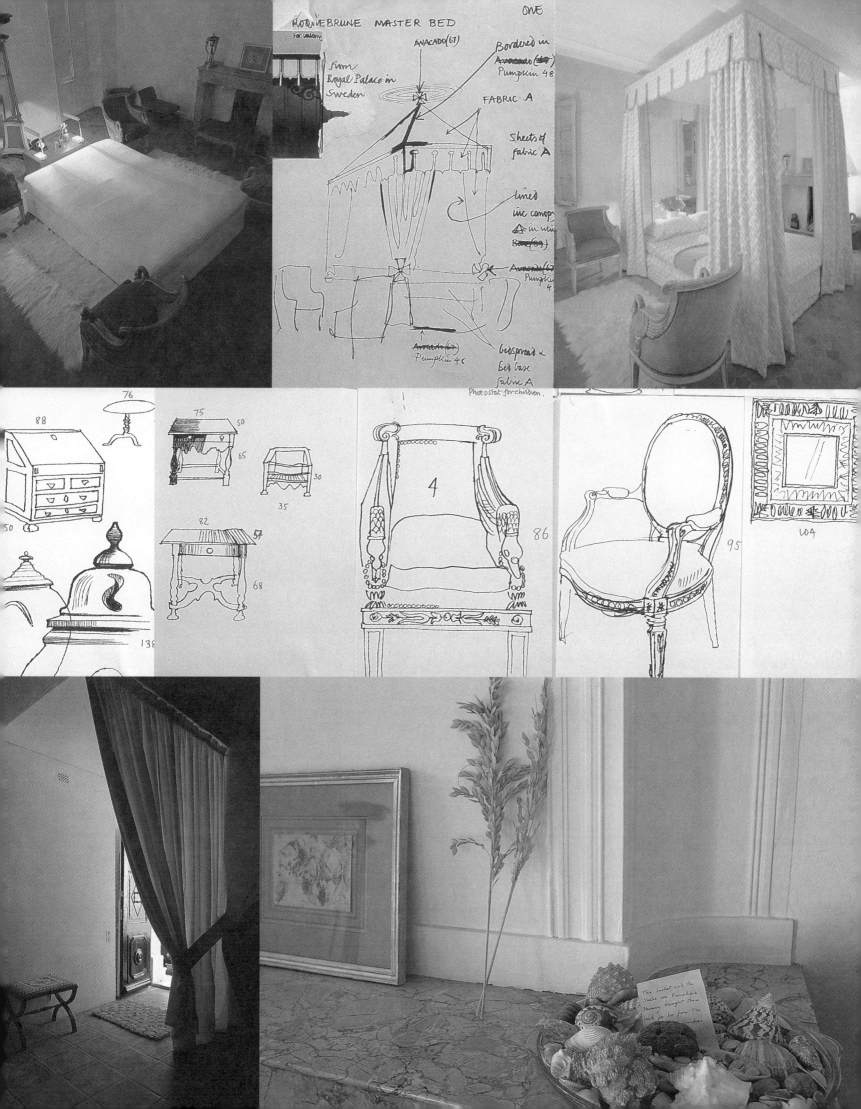

'For Sale' – the house in Roquebrune as my father found it in 1966.

The Roquebrune dining room with a Joe Tilson plastic relief mixed with an old brass chandelier and local chairs.

A bedroom at Savannah, with 'floating' concrete table and lobster silhouettes in gouache by the Hicks studio.

Added to these ingredients were eclectic pieces, such as a heavily weathered wooden Buddha which sat up on a table surrounded by shell necklaces, and a few modern chairs. He also bought some wonderful things in towns near there, like a very unusual 1800 chimneypiece for the hall in marbleized pottery from Apt. Soon afterwards, he bought an old workshop in a street nearby, with a yard at the back where he built a swimming pool. The workshop became changing rooms and a big studio room that gave on to the pool. The walls of the changing rooms were left in the roughest, most jagged cement, on which we children hurt ourselves as we changed. But I remember the beautiful contrast of the rough wall with the immaculate hanging curtains of white cotton that divided the space.

Eleuthera

My parents had been to the Bahamas first on honeymoon, staying in Nassau and then on the beautiful out-island of Eleuthera, named after the Greek word for 'freedom' by its first European settlers. This wonderful island of pink-coral sand beaches and simple native villages attracted them immediately and, when in the late 1960s they were able to buy a plot of land on one of the beaches, they jumped at the chance. My father was in a sun-worshipping mood and working a great deal in New York, regularly going down to Nassau to stay with friends. At the time, as it happened, a director of one of the big American airlines had a house on Eleuthera and had arranged a daily flight from New York to the local airport, so that from the St Regis it took him only four hours to get to the beach.

My father, like so many aesthetes before him, had always loved all things Egyptian, starting with his grandfather's old marble clock with its gilded sphinx and his father's jewelled Freemason's badge. My mother and he had been to Egypt a few years before and he had, of course, photographed everything, but the monument that excited him most of all was the severe, totally modern-looking complex of King Zoser at Saqqâra. In 1969, in collaboration with a talented Nassau architect, Robert Stokes, he drew up plans for a modern beach house inspired by this millennia-old monument. The first sketches are much more elaborate than the end result, with a swimming pool and two storeys. In the end, the house was built on one floor only, with the only water being two small, dripping fountains on free-standing 'pylons' in front of a screened loggia dining room.

The finished house – named Savannah after the nearby village of pretty, painted wooden houses – was a triumph. It stood back from the beach, up on a small hill with views of the Atlantic on one side and the narrow Savannah Sound on the other. The walls both inside and out were rendered with rough cement, made with the pink sand of the beach and scored with nails on a board in order to give them a lively, textured look. The floors were made in the same way. All of the doors were made with fixed panels above, so that they appeared to be full height, vanishing into the floating ceilings of white plaster. The French doors to outside were all specially made in bronzed aluminium.

The interior was decorated very simply. The bedrooms had bedside tables made in cement like the walls, floating blocks with lights within that lit the floor. Everywhere there were Hicks fabrics printed in soft pastel colours on heavy, rough linen. The living room was dominated by a pair of big, abstract paintings by Bruce Tippett – a young artist who had been sent to study in Rome at my parents' expense, in return for these paintings and another that hung over the chimney at Britwell. Others of these scroll-topped canvases appeared in several of my father's jobs in those years, with their colours specified to work with the scheme. The living room had a large fireplace, which was used only once (because it smoked) but gave the room a very grand feeling, with driftwood from the beach stacked up within it.

Fierce air conditioning was kept on when my father was inside. He would go up to the pool at the nearby club and grill himself under the scorching Bahamian sun, then return to the house, where he would keep all the windows tight shut. There – the air chilled, a cigarette in his hands and a large drink with his big American ice cubes, and military music like 'Pomp and Circumstance' playing at immense volume on the stereo – he would pace the room contentedly. In the evening, we would all sit at the dining table on the large, screened porch, sketching as the sun set in a flood of incredible colour, reflected in the water of Savannah Sound, exactly between the twin pylons that fronted the house. King Zoser never had it so good.

My uncle and aunt bought the neighbouring plot, right on the beach, and built themselves an utterly typical Bahamian holiday house, using the same architect but none of the same ideas. They had pretty, painted tile floors and delightful headboards on the beds, giant peacocks in bright turquoise raffia. As children, we would go from one house to the other and marvel at the differences. In one way, of course, we loved the other house, where the sea breeze blew through all day, the air was never chilled, and one could run about and be as noisy as one liked – quite different from our house, where my father was busily pursuing his curious vision of a stylish life. But it was not only our fierce pride in our father's obvious genius that made us prefer our own house; its beauty was clear to us all. Every comment from our charmingly philistine cousins only made us more proud of it.

St Jean

The drawback of the French house in Roquebrune was the drive to the sea, which was very pretty but took longer every year as the area became more popular and traffic increased. We had a speedboat named, in a pun on the French pronunciation of 'Hicks', *Les X*, which we kept at Fréjus for waterskiing or just going out to swim in the sea. The boat, of course, had a flag with the 'H' logo (which was flown at all times) and Hicks-designed towels with a pattern of the same motif (which I have now used for the cover of this book). In order to avoid this drive, we sold the house in 1973 and found something in St Jean, Cap Ferrat, a small, new house in a modern terrace of white concrete. Here we kept the boat in the little harbour and had merely to walk five minutes to it from the house.

The house could not have been more different from the charming old town house in Roquebrune. This was 1970s international concrete, all awkward-shaped, small rooms and asymmetrical balconies. On the other hand, it presented a challenge that the other house did not have. To make something beautiful out of a horror is always exciting, and this was no exception. With every new house, the Hicks style developed and moved on, responding to the times but also to an internal sense of a progress within his work. Here he rather self-consciously avoided pattern, using only plain fabrics in the very spare interior that he created, with clear, bright colours that were rather his look at the time, colours influenced in part by the pretty Caribbean houses of the villages in the Bahamas.

The old wooden Buddha came with us from Roquebrune and sat up on a table in the window of the new living room at the front of the house. I recall one of our neighbours asking, fascinated, whether it was my father who meditated every evening, up there in the window – she was amazed to come upstairs and see the sculpture sitting there. The house was half the size of Roquebrune, and here my bedroom (which had in the old house been a good size, with a battlemented tester bed with Hicks sheets as hangings) was a long cupboard next to the

At the newly finished Savannah, 1970; very hip, but also hot, in a local straw hat and black leather jacket.

Savannah in construction, from the beach side, and looking very King Zoser-like.

The living room at St Jean – yellow, pink and turquoise, with the wooden Buddha on the table in the window.

Lord Mountbatten's cypher, carved in stone at his Classiebawn Castle, Ireland.

The author with his grandfather, at Classiebawn Castle, 1969.

The Hicks-designed changing rooms for the new swimming pool at Broadlands, 1970, in red-and-white striped canvas.

kitchen, with a bunk into which I would crawl to sleep. A little hot on occasion, but I pretended it was on a yacht and was happy enough.

While we were in France as a family, which was generally for three weeks at the start of the summer, my father would take me to see things nearby, working on a kind of artistic education for which I am now grateful. There is a lot to see within a small area, and we would go every year to the Fondation Maeght, to the Villa Kerylos at Beaulieu (past which I would also waterski, which I loved), to the great Roman Triomphe des Alpes at la Turbie. We would draw together, both seriously and for fun, when we would all play Heads, Bottoms and Tails, that charming game where each person draws part of a figure, the rest of which is folded away.

For St Jean, as for every house, one of the first excitements was designing a new writing paper. Few things gave my father quite such pleasure in life as did a new writing paper. Part of the look of each house, he would consider its design every bit as carefully as any other element of the decor. St Jean had that delicate turquoise colour so typical of the Bahamian village houses, with white writing in a very 1970s typeface. Something similar – but in a pink again, typical of Eleuthera, with the address in a rust colour – was made for our new London apartment in Paulton's Square. The fascination that writing paper held for him was enormous: he was never without a large collection of other people's paper in his briefcase, and loved to abstract the grander kind from grand houses.

As a young man without money, but with dreams and ambition, he spent a lot of his time at the Central School of Art studying graphic design. On the back of many of his student book jackets are sketched designs for writing papers, mostly decorated with elaborate coronets. There are innumerable sketched-out invitations ('Mr David Hicks requests the pleasure of the company…') from when he

was about 15. The taste for graphics never left him, making writing papers for his houses and for his business (some for clients too), matchbooks with his 'H' logo, our luggage labels, signs for the various houses on the country estate, promotional brochures for the business and all of his books, which were designed by others but very much under his direction.

'Tweed, jokes, stories, castles, estates…'

Like a lot of other things in his life, my father's interest in graphics and smart presentation was fuelled enormously by his father-in-law. Lord Mountbatten was not one of those who shrugs off his status and is understated in his lifestyle, and the precision with which his cypher, his coat of arms and everything else in his life was designed was of keen interest to him. Being the artistic grandchild, I was often ordered to come out to Ireland or the Bahamas with waterproof paints to repair a faded flag that had flown over his house too long, or instructed to copy the design of his cypher on to tracing paper (a monogram of 'M of B', for his title, Mountbatten of Burma, within the Garter, surmounted by his earl's coronet), to be sent off to whomever had volunteered to make him some new needlepoint slippers.

My father was also called on to provide services occasionally, as when he designed very amusing changing rooms for my grandfather's new swimming pool at Broadlands. The rooms were built inside a red-and-white-striped 'tent' with gold spear finials, like something from a medieval tournament inserted within the distinguished eighteenth-century orangery. My grandfather, who was never overpleased with my mother's choice of husband, nonetheless did have a grudging admiration for the quality of my father's work and never missed an opportunity to support him in any way possible. It meant a great deal to my father to receive letters from his father-in-law praising whichever new job he had seen, whether the nightclub on the *QE2* liner, the revolving restaurant atop London's GPO Tower or the newest David Hicks shop, the openings of which he invariably attended.

For my father, always being labelled 'Lord Mountbatten's son-in-law' was a cross that he bore with marked resilience. He did, of course, owe a great deal of his publicity and newsworthiness to this position, which he was the first to acknowledge. On the other hand, he remembered only too well the year or more without work that immediately followed his marriage, and knew that plenty of potential clients throughout his career were frightened away by the intimidating prospect of such a well-connected, well-known decorator. On the whole, it was a mixed blessing, but he did find it hard that, no matter how hard he worked and how well-known his work became, he could never escape being, foremost in so many people's minds, the son-in-law.

Being around him so much, I am sure, made my father more and more fascinated by every detail of my grandfather's extraordinary life and reflect much of it in his own. Always ambitious, the real fire to succeed and to wrap the world in David Hicks came from the presence in his life of my towering, extraordinarily famous grandfather. He was determined to prove himself and make his father-in-law as proud of his son-in-law as he was of him, for he was certainly proud of being married to Lady Pamela Mountbatten. He never quite outgrew the boy from Essex, and woke every morning in mild self-congratulation at his own good fortune in being her husband.

I came across a scribbled note, written over the agenda of a meeting in 1976, which seems to list the qualities that came to his mind when thinking of my mother's family: 'Tweed, jokes, stories, castles, estates, jewels; family, Saint, cake, German, Russian, Swedish, Greek and Bulgarian relations; uniforms, liveries, privately printed books, mascot, cyphers and descent from Charlemagne and Pocahontas.' Why *those* qualities, why *then*? Why list them at all? I can no longer ask him, but what does come across in the list, as in everything he wrote and said and did in relation to her family, is his huge aesthetic enjoyment of it, and his fierce pride at having a place within it...or almost within it.

It was inevitable that my father would not really fit into my mother's family. He had always been at the centre of his own world, elevated by his mother to an unassailable position; and suddenly he found, instead, that he was merely a minor planet revolving around a greater sun. Try as he could to fit in, it was useless, for he could never achieve their utter disdain for the world around them, the world from which he himself had come. He could shoot their birds and ride their horses, he could dress in their tweeds and laugh at their stories – even work for them without payment – but to no avail. He always remained the outsider.

The long family holidays, especially the month in Ireland every summer – with its routine of fishing, riding and dam-building on the beach, my grandfather surrounded by his ten grandchildren – did tend to drag for my father, whose idea of fun was somewhat different. He would drive off for days, touring the country, looking at every decaying Irish mansion he could find, returning to thrill us with tales of eccentric peers whose drawing rooms were carpeted with straw for their horses' comfort. When he stayed with us, he would busy himself with his briefcase, working on plans and schemes or writing endless letters.

One of these, written in July 1972, was in response to a plaintive letter from old clients and friends for whom he was decorating a London apartment after successfully finishing their country house. The clients had complained that their new living room 'has no zip or style, it simply is

Press cuttings dwelling, as always, on my father's royal connections.

My father (right) 'fitting in' out shooting, 1971, with his brother-in-law, father-in-law, sister-in-law and a nephew.

Hicks takes aim.

The new Rolls-Royce in the snow at Britwell, 1971.

My grandfather, Herbert Hicks, in his robes as Master of the Salters Company.

not David Hicks'. He replied, on his father-in-law's grandly cypher-decorated Classiebawn Castle writing paper, between snippets of holiday news:

You are both very civilised and sympathetic human beings with very much in common with ourselves and that's why not only do I value your friendship but I want what I do for you NOW to be as satisfactory as what I did previously. There really isn't very much difference except that before it was a beautiful, sympathetic country house while Grosvenor Square is a pig! of a flat…

I love spending other people's money – if it is spent well – and will go out shopping with you any time you want. But not window shopping! I don't take your letter at all amiss. We all need criticism and the day I can't take it I'll be finished. Take it from me here and now that I'll get that room so right you won't be able to tear yourselves away from it.

Keeping up with the Mountbattens

My father's search for a life stylish enough to compare with all of this Mountbatten glory took many forms. Among the unfortunate aspects of this was his egotism. He was a person of very great significance in his own mind, and was known to say some absurd things. Famous photographer Norman Parkinson had come to do a picture of my sister India (as a royal bridesmaid) for the cover of *Tatler*, and made the mistake of asking my father for some fusewire, to tie some flowers into India's hair. He barked indignantly at Parkinson, 'Do I look like a man who mends his own fuses?' Any journalist who went to interview him and had not 'done their homework' was very unpopular, and he would refuse to give details of his career to date, since they were readily available with a little research.

With advancing years, these traits became more marked, and his impatience more extreme. People invited for lunch at 1.15p.m., who were anyway having to drive more than an hour from London for the privilege, would be greeted with stony-faced fury by their host if they arrived after 1p.m. From 12.30p.m. onwards he would be pacing the hall, noisily complaining already of how late they would be, lamenting the quality of modern guests and how he himself would never do any such thing. I remember one unfortunate couple, who came for lunch on what they were sure was the right Saturday, only to be summarily dismissed by my father, who swore he had said the next week and instructed them to return on the correct date.

Anyone who got it right, however – anyone who was on time and clever enough to have looked through an old Hicks book or two, or merely made the right kind of appreciative comments while being shown the garden and house – was richly rewarded with great, smothering waves of charm. These guests were a delight ('highly intelligent' was always the description of anyone who was ready to flatter just a little), and they were, in turn, delighted by him. He would turn his attention full on them, charming and beguiling them, praising their complexion, gently criticizing their outfit, making them laugh with his wonderful, infectious humour, finding just the right rose from his 'Secret Garden' for their buttonhole, or a whole posy of them to take back to London.

Every aspect of his life was an aesthetic gesture. When I was a child, his cars were a great expression of Hicks style. The first that I recall was a stately 1963 Mercedes, with smoked glass in the back and a huge, early form of car telephone, which was mainly used to alert the butler at Britwell that he was about to arrive. Not a great success… Thereafter my father had two firm views on what he called motorcars – smoked glass is strictly for pop stars only, and mobile telephones are nothing but a nuisance. The smoked glass was a great feature of the times, however, and his regency drawing-room windows in St Leonard's Terrace were fitted with it 'as a defence against the dreary greyness of London light'.

There followed a succession of Rolls-Royces and E-type Jaguars, each more exciting than the last, for both him and his motor-obsessed son. He was fiercely jealous of my grandfather's immensely stylish cars, which were distinctively painted pale blue with a black roof (as they had always been since his wedding in 1922) and with a large silver mascot of a sailor signalling 'LM' in miniature semaphore flags. The mascot had been a wedding present from the Prince of Wales, later Duke of Windsor. Who could possibly rival the chic of that combination? Try my father did, though, and one strange idea (an economy measure of the mid-1970s) was to replace the Rolls with two identical Peugeot saloons, each painted black with small gold 'H' logos on the doors, and interiors specially done all in black felt.

My grandfather, Herbert Hicks, as well as being a keen Freemason, had been twice Master of the Worshipful Company of Salters, one of the twelve great livery companies of the City of London. Hickses had been in the company for several generations, and this was the one hereditary spark of glory that my father could claim. It was not much compared to my mother's ancestral roster – which included Charlemagne, two saints and Lady Godiva, not to mention the endless royalties catalogued in exhausting detail by my grandfather in his 'relationship tables', modelled on a horse breeders' stud book – but at the Salters my father was on the Court, as four Hicks generations had been before him. He even managed to be Master in the year of the Queen's Silver Jubilee, inviting his sovereign to tea at Salters' Hall, where he – for once in his life – would not have to stay a pace behind his wife, or ten paces behind his father-in-law.

From the age of 40, he loved the Salters, and was always there for Court lunch on Thursday, mulling over the details of the wine, the display of silver plate or the redecoration of the Master's apartment. The hall, a fine Regency building, was destroyed in the War, and the new building by Sir Basil Spence, in a high-modern Scandinavian style, took all of Hicks's genius to transform into a space worthy of the grand dinners held there. He especially delighted in redesigning the Court robes, which he (as Master and then Past Master) wore with evident pleasure. In the instructions for his funeral, he was very precise that, not only should the Salters' Court process, but that the Beadle, their butler, should lead them with his silver staff of office. The scarlet robes, with their royal-blue and ermine edging, made a wonderful splash of colour against the green churchyard, just as he had planned, making an unusually beautiful page in *Hello!* magazine.

One of the most amusing things I discovered while going through my father's papers after his death was a series of notes 'for the Venetian Palazzo'. He had obviously decided that life was not properly complete without one, and was busily designing every detail, down to the special gondola posts outside it with jazzy Hicks colours and an 'H' logo, and a flag of similar design 'for Venetian motor-launch'. There are, too, scribbled notes reminding him to get his secretary to work on the butler's uniform for Venice. They must be from around 1970. So far as I know, he had not found a property there, and certainly he never mentioned it, so I imagine it was a very short-lived fantasy. How typical of him, though, to be already working on the graphics of those key details, which would have made the 'Palazzo Hicks' the epicentre of life on the Grand Canal!

Salters' Hall in the City of London. The walls are blond wood, made dramatic by my father's dynamic lighting.

Hicks and Parr

My father was an inveterate shopkeeper. He loved to have a shop, a window, a showroom for his work, an outlet for his style. He would say that there was no point sitting in an office waiting for word-of-mouth contacts to bring in work when a shop window would produce new clients. Many of his early impressions of glamour and style were from shops, like the childhood, wartime visits to Fortnum & Mason, which 'was wonderfully grand in those days…the customers were all women in mink coats, with wonderful, clanking gold bracelets and chains. There was such an atmosphere of luxury in the shop.'

When he was passing through London, on army leave to see his mama in East Anglia, he would go and press his nose against shop windows. One day he was bold enough to go into Syrie Maugham's shop. Inside was a commanding woman with a long, three-quarter-length, navy-blue dress and a big hat. She was shouting at someone, 'Send the lamps round at once! Her Ladyship wants them now!', which he thought was absolutely wonderful. A friend of his mother, who happened to be there, said, 'Hello! Aren't you Iris Hicks's son?,' and introduced him to Syrie Maugham. 'That's the only time I met her,' he told me. 'She didn't have charm or glamour or chic, but I suppose she had a certain style.'

Roy Alderson, a King's Road antique dealer in the 1950s, had very entertaining windows that he changed weekly. The great entertainment after dinner was to go and look at Roy's windows. One of the best had a stag sitting up in bed – 'in fact a stag in drag', he told me, 'because it was wearing ropes and ropes of pearls and a wig. It was having tea out of a marvellous cup and reading a nineteenth-century newspaper. It was always mad and fun.' Alderson had a famous dining room in his flat above the shop. They would have drinks, and then their host would say, 'Come and stand over by the fire.' He'd crank a handle, and a dining table with fold-down legs would come down. When dinner was over, he would wind the table back up on to the ceiling. The underside was painted to look like an Adam ceiling.

In 1956, two years after his first success, when his house appeared in *House & Garden*, my father opened his first shop, in partnership with Tom Parr. They had met while Tom was working at the General Trading Company, with my father's cousin Elizabeth Everard, then head of the GTC's china department, for which my father designed a new showroom (his first venture into retail design). He then went on to do windows for the GTC. Tom and he had a very successful partnership for four years, until they parted and Tom went on quietly to create the great international success of Colefax & Fowler.

He was staying one weekend at Vaynol, Sir Michael Duff's huge house in north Wales. The house had marvellous silver, a coal fire in his bathroom and a wood fire in his bedroom – it was run in that prewar way. Tom Parr was also staying there. It was a lovely morning, so the two went for a walk in the park. My father said, 'You know, you ought to have an antique shop and I ought to have a decorating shop. Why don't we get something together?' They were very excited about this idea and announced it to the house party at lunch, who loved the idea of 'Hicks and Parr'. They found a shop in 'absolutely the right part of the world', opposite Hotspur, a famous antique shop which always had the finest English furniture.

Hicks designed the shop, and then Hicks and Parr both went off buying furniture as stock. My father ordered new sofas and some chairs, they bought secondhand lamps and made new shades for them, and went on a sweep of England, buying 'lots of really marvellous things

'Turkish Tulip', an early fabric inspired by an Ottoman velvet in the Topkapi, Istanbul.

very inexpensively, and priced them up no end'. They had a big opening party, with a crowd of grand people whom they knew, the sort of people who would talk about the new shop. It went well, because Tom was very good with figures. The shop was full of exciting furniture, porcelain, engravings, and in the window they placed a pair of Chippendale chairs, covered in horsehair, which 'everybody raved about as it hadn't been seen for a hundred years'.

Carpets and Fabrics

Whereas most decorators spend their whole working lives using existing materials, once in a while recolouring something, while a few of them find old things and have them specially reprinted or woven, my father almost from the beginning was unwilling to restrict himself in this way. He had, after all, trained as a designer and artist – most unusual in those days when the average decorator had no training of any kind beyond working for someone else. Even on his first house in South Eaton Place in 1954, he had found old printing blocks for 1890s wallpapers and had these printed in his own colours. Out of despair at the paucity of interesting patterned fabric, and consciously avoiding the John Fowler chintz look, he used none at all, sticking instead with plains.

In 1961, when decorating Britwell, he had his first geometric carpets woven, after designs adapted from tilework he had photographed in Isfahan. In 1963, for his own bedroom in London, he designed his first fabric, a rough, modern interpretation of traditional florals, tumbling abstract flowers printed in vivid reds, pinks and yellows, which covered walls, curtains and bed in a startling, psychedelic rose bower. The next fabrics were mainly geometrics and very stylized – formal florals, adapted from different historical sources (Egyptian, Indian, Turkish) as his eye wandered across the huge pages of his first-edition Owen Jones *Grammar of Ornament*, which always sat by his desk in our London house or apartment, its more geometric pages covered with little pencil notes addressed to his studio, whose task it was to adapt the old designs to his specifications.

My grandfather Lord Mountbatten was amazed when he was told that his son-in-law was designing a collection of plain fabrics for a Yorkshire textile firm. He could not believe for a moment that 'hard-headed Yorkshiremen' could be persuaded to pay a London designer simply to choose colours and name them. Today, with thousands of such collections in design showrooms around the world, no one would be surprised, but in 1967 it did seem quite revolutionary. The colours were shockingly strong at the time, and I think the collections sold only their muted beige tones to other customers. It was the David Hicks clients who bought 'Red Rag' and 'Simply Scarlet'. Even 'Colonel Mustard' was too strong for ordinary mortals.

It was his commercial clients, the growing numbers of international David Hicks Associates and the customers of Harmony Carpet and Connaissance Fabrics (the US distributors of his designs) who used the standard colourways, whether muted or shrill. Instead, in his private work my father very often printed these designs in his favourite thick, opaque white paste on heavy, rough canvas or natural linen, occasionally instead using one of the coloured wools as base, like two emerald-green bedrooms for different clients in the early 1970s. He loved the look of this – the painterly feel of the solid white print on the coarse cloth – and used the formula again and again. In all of his work, he used a lot of white, which sharpened up and grounded the colours, rather as the very graphic white outlines had done in his early gouaches of Italy.

My father was interested in product design from an early stage and very quickly in the 1960s began to look at new forms and new pieces. Furniture was a crowded field

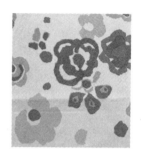

'Tumbling Roses', the first torn-paper floral design.

'Chevron', here a wallpaper in piercing lime green, black and dark olive.

One of two bedrooms entirely covered in Hicks Indian, printed in white impasto on coarse emerald-green 'tweed'.

'Octagon', an early geometric carpet design.

Three geometrics: 'Hicksonian', 'Crossbridge' and 'Queen Bee'.

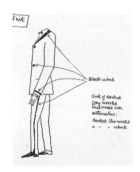

One of the David Hicks for Daks sketches, 1969.

A sketch for one of the David Hicks sculptures, exhibited together with his portrait drawings.

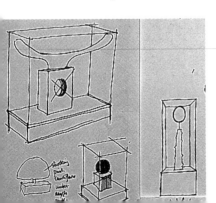

and consequently he only made a few commissioned pieces for specific jobs, and one or two things that were sold through his shops. The pieces that he did make were hard-edged, modern, uncompromising, but beautifully proportioned so that they sat easily alongside fine antique pieces. He made Perspex cubes, in white, red, bright yellow. He made tables inspired by Jean-Michel Frank, with tiny squares of lizard skin stitched together covering a Parsons table shape. He made desks and side-tables with chromed steel trestles holding a thick glass top. Every one of these pieces was simplicity itself.

Early on, he started on lamps, ashtrays, smaller accessories that would give the shops easy items to sell, which went on to include photograph frames, trays and books covered in Hicks fabrics. The accessories were an ideal way to give the DH signature to an interior that had been compromised by clients' reluctance and dithering. They also gave admirers an easy way to add just a touch of Hicks style to their home. His eye and hand were always restless, and encountering ugly, badly designed objects throughout the day (outside his own home or office, of course) spurred him to improve on them in ways that were sometimes realized, sometimes not.

Intriguing finds that I made recently include a sketched collection of men's clothes for Daks from around 1969 – never produced, but very chic, and very much of their time. I also found a whole sheaf of sketches for David Hicks sculptures, some of which *were* made. These were exhibited along with his portraits, a Warhol-esque venture in which he photographed his family, friends and various celebrities, and then had his studio make black dot prints of them by hand. Today this would take a moment with a computer, but then must have kept his design staff busy for weeks. The exhibition was not, I think, a great success: quite a lot of the portraits did not sell, although the sculptures found homes in his projects, a few ending up in our house in the Bahamas. One of these sculptures was four old-fashioned dish mops, standing in a wooden base under a Perspex case like four stylized palm trees. These had to be replaced a couple of times, when our Bahamian maid had put them to a more practical use.

David Hicks on...

'David Hicks revolutionised the floors of the world with his geometric carpets', wrote his great friend and counterpart, New York decorator Billy Baldwin, who used several of them in his own work, notably in the Harding-Lawrences' dining room at La Fiorentina. Baldwin's outspoken books on decorating were very similar in spirit to my father's, and are now equally sought-after. The two designers ran a mutual admiration society for a while, with my father dedicating his fourth book, the 1971 *David Hicks on Decoration – with Fabrics*, 'To William Baldwin and John Fowler with admiration'. Baldwin wrote to thank my father for this compliment but unfortunately said that he was proud of him, which was taken badly by my father (who thought it patronising, suggesting that he owed something to the American). They argued over this until my father was persuaded by his patient, adoring wife to write what was clearly intended as an apology:

Dear Billy
Your charming letter cannot go unanswered because I don't want you to think I feel that we ever disagree! What I mean is that I know we see eye to eye about practically everything but do you drink white wine with every meal as I do? Do I like Kitty as much as you do? Do you put up with shooting bores as I do? It's minutiae – you are five minutes older than I am – you are American and I am English – which is what makes it so extraordinary that we do agree on a billion things to my mind.

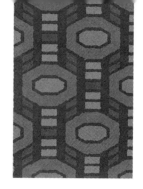

A later torn-paper design, made as printed fabric and as textured carpet, 1974.

But it needs conversation, not a letter. You say, and I know genuinely, the nicest things about my new book and I shall keep your letter always. I so appreciate your saying you are proud of me because you have shown and taught me so much. Longing for your visit in May.

Yours ever, David

If they made up, it was temporary. I well remember hearing my father object that a decorating magazine was still interested in the man: 'Billy Baldwin, that pompous old bore, didn't have a shred of originality in his whole body.' Doubtless, time would have healed the rift as it did so many others, if time there had been.

In all, my father published twelve books, including the *Highland Clans* that he did in collaboration with Sir Iain Moncreiffe of that ilk, and his *My Kind of Garden* (which I completed after his death), on which he had been working for ten years. All of these books – but especially the original series of five *David Hicks on...* and the comprehensive *Living with Design* – must be among the most-used designers' resources in the world, referred to as frequently in many decorating studios as Owen Jones's *Grammar of Ornament* was in my father's. Many was the time that he would wander into a designer's office, whether in Madrid, Bangkok or Seattle, to find one of his books lying open on a desk. Still today, thirty-five years later – especially today – *David Hicks on...* is inspiring, informing and supplying the world's designers, in both home and fashion.

The strong design of most of the books was the work of Nicholas Jenkins, a very talented and eminent graphic designer, whose main work was a large portfolio of retail corporate images, the smallest of which was the David Hicks shop in 1977. When I was 15, I watched Nick and my father put *Living with Design* together, which I was proud to have contributed to in the shape of several pages of my photographs of classical architectural details. I was fascinated to sit with them as, tape recorder running, Nick would produce picture layouts and my father would improvise – quite unprepared and impromptu, without ever correcting himself and barely pausing – 'It is sometimes interesting to use the raw materials of a house...' or 'Any room that has a fireplace should be planned around it...'

All of these books were written in this way, with my father dictating to a secretary, writer or designer, and then correcting a series of typed-up drafts, usually making use of my mother (herself a very talented, never-published writer) as editor. On one occasion – for an unpublished *Textbook of Interior Design* that developed into the 1987 *Style & Design* – he did write text himself, but it emerged ponderous and self-conscious, without any of the flair of his unrehearsed, spoken thoughts. Curiously enough, he in fact wrote a good deal, and I have files full of wonderful, vivid descriptions of people and places, particularly of any royal events and visits, which are all beautifully written. Among the stranger fragments is the first chapter of a novel (typically him – a Firbank or Mitford for the 1970s), which was abandoned, no doubt, as soon as the aeroplane's wheels hit the Heathrow runway and his thoughts turned back to work.

David Hicks and...

Having closed his first shop in 1963, my father of course yearned for another, and very soon, with a lot of products to sell and only so many clients to sell to, retail beckoned again. A succession of London ventures followed, in partnership with a whole variety of friends and collaborators, all of them in that small, fashionable stretch of Chelsea that persists to this day. One of the high points was David Hicks + Zarach, with Neil Zarach, who went on

'Zed', one of the geometrics used for sheeting and towels by J. P. Stevens, 1971.

Another torn-paper floral, 1971.

'Indian' recoloured as a carpet in burnt orange, mustard and scarlet on a seaweed ground, 1976.

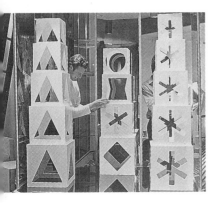

Arranging playful étagères *in white perspex for the opening of David Hicks + Zarach on the Fulham Road, 1970.*

A David Hicks reading stand in white formica for the bath, with – what else? – a David Hicks book, 1970.

At the David Hicks + Zarach opening party, a glowing David Hicks all in white.

to have a very exciting shop on South Audley Street for many years. Their shop was wildly stylish and very 1967 – entirely black and white, with acres of white or transparent plastic furniture designed by Hicks and made by his friend Michael Severne, who continued to produce Perspex or Lucite pieces for him for thirty years.

The rather polite opening of Hicks and Parr ten years before gave way to a newsworthy, chic 'White Opening', where anyone not dressed in white was turned away. The star of the evening was Zarach's Swedish secretary in a white crochet bikini, who lasted about two weeks. The combination of modern style and old society was perfect, with Margaret, Duchess of Argyll caught (for *Vogue*) deep in conversation with Prince Ali of Murshidabad on the DH geometric carpet. The objects and furniture in the shop were also marketed through a showroom in Paris – the first venture abroad, which was brief, but it did pave the way for things to come.

The most enduring of these shops, and the one that I remember the best, was David Hicks Mary Fox-Linton, in the very same building on Chelsea Green where Allegra and I have just now, thirty years later, opened her first, tiny retail outlet. I so well recall visits there, before or after lunch at the wonderful Don Luigi on the King's Road. We would jump up and down on the doormat – which rang a bell to warn of a customer's appearance – and no doubt we drove the poor staff crazy. Mary Fox-Linton went on to work on very stylish and important projects, such as the No. 1 Aldwych Hotel, and still runs the best fabric showroom in London.

The shop was always crowded with pretty things and was very much a shop, without contrived room-settings but with fabrics and carpet samples in abundance. The colours were cheerful and bright, with much of that Eleuthera village influence, a very clean look. They sold a large number of Indian dhurries in pastel shades, and wonderful Tapis de Cogolin, textured white carpet from Provence, of which my father designed a collection at the time. There were still the plastic accessories, but they were more muted, less hard-edged, with the small geometric prints included in the plastic and also made up into notebooks and albums.

At this point in time, the business was changing direction, aiming more and more towards larger, commercial projects and doing less private work. I am sure that this had a negative effect on my father's creativity and his inspiration, for the work produced by the firm became gradually more predictable, more commercial-looking, less adventurous. It was a slow process, but an inexorable one. My father always refused to believe that he could ever understand business (or indeed anything to do with money) besides get discounts from suppliers, who were often induced to give their wares for free, for the publicity value they would get from his using them. Every little sketch and doodle, every reflective note for a future autobiography, every one of these is on the minutes of a meeting, the agenda illegible, obscured by a sketched flag for his new boat.

This deliberate, conscious decision to be an artist, to be solely creative, not even to attempt to understand his business position, on the one hand freed him to create full time, without any distraction; on the other, it meant that he lost any control over the direction of the business, becoming a passenger in his own vehicle. In the early years, this was good, freeing his time, unleashing his talent, without restriction, but later it throttled him. More and more he came to see the management of the business as an outside force over which he had no control and for which he had no responsibility. The roots of this tendency were deep, deriving from his childhood loss of house and possessions after his mother had entrusted everything to a useless cousin. Its effects were equally long-lasting.

The Last Shop

In 1978, my father realised his dream of a grand new showroom, with offices and design studio all in the same building. To show how very established and mature the business was, this happened not in Chelsea (where they had been for twenty years) but in Jermyn Street, home of more traditional English men's shops than any other street, supplying shirts, cigars, wines, old masters and antiquities to the customers of the tailors on nearby Savile Row.

This was the new image of David Hicks. He and the business, both of which had always thrived on novelty and innovation, were settling comfortably into middle age. Everything about the new setup was impressive, with long windows on Jermyn Street, his name writ large and alone above the door, four complete room-sets in the front of the shop, separated by a vast 'H' logo laid out on the floor in dark wood and coconut matting, with further sets in the back and downstairs. No expense was spared in making this the defining and absolute statement of his style. In fact, of course, by now he was left with so little time to give to each project that, in reality, he designed almost nothing.

At the time, he was fortunate in having a very talented young designer, Paul Hull, to direct the design and decoration of the shop and most of their projects. The shop, with even more space in the basement – which fabric and carpet displays, a large bathroom set and an enormous living room scarcely filled – was crowded with Hicks-designed products, lamps, ashtrays, furniture, and other items carefully chosen to work with the style. There were always abstract paintings by Rib Bloomfield, whose very particular style fitted the look of both shop and projects so well that almost no DH interior was without one of his paintings then.

Passing through the shop, an imposing-looking stair led up between white-painted wooden grilles, behind which accountants busily added numbers, to the master's lair at the back, a minimalist white box of an office, its window of frosted glass covered with another white grille, quite empty apart from the large, square desk of white melamine with four scarlet, tweed-covered high-backed chairs around it. The desk was divided (with ebony bands in graphic, Hicks style) into nine squares, some of which opened to reveal drawers or in- and out-trays. It was his rendering of his honeymoon visit to Philip Johnson, and it had the desired, intimidating effect on visitors.

A growing business in Japan, licensing the David Hicks name to a wide variety of manufacturers of home and fashion goods, led to a whole studio of product designers setting up alongside the fabric and carpet designers who had always worked up my father's sketches and ideas. Some of the Japanese products were, and are (for the business continues today) marvellous, while others are so particularly aimed at the Japanese market that they do not translate well abroad. My father was very proud of the pop-up, miniature umbrellas covered with his 'H'-logo patterns and of an amazing pinstripe suit on which, close inspection revealed, each stripe was in fact his signature strung together: 'David Hicks, David Hicks, David…'

Inspired by the Japanese business, and in order to support the fashion side of it, the company ventured into women's fashion. Unlike the sketch designs from 1969 for Daks menswear, however, the collection had 'no zip or style, it simply is not David Hicks' (as that disgruntled London client had complained about his living room). The fashion collections seemed aimed at middle-aged female executives, who might well have been the most likely customers but were certainly not inspiring muses. After three expensive and frustrating seasons, they disappeared, but not before my father had hugely enjoyed presenting small runway shows in the shop itself, introducing the outfits to the strains of Grace Jones's 'Am I Ever Gonna Fall in Love in New York City?'

The severe, bronze-aluminium front of the last David Hicks shop on Jermyn Street, 1978.

The stairs up to DH's office at the back of the last shop, Jermyn Street, 1978.

Presenting new fabric designs to the David Hicks Association of Japanese Manufacturers, Tokyo, 1977.

Europe

Following his adventure in the United States, from 1973 my father's focus shifted more and more towards Europe as the potential growth area for his activities. Perhaps in a way he was returning to the excitement of that first journey aged 17 to sun-filled, lavender-scented Provence. More pragmatically, dispirited by the difficulty of controlling the exploitation of his designs in the USA, it seemed sensible to regroup nearer home shores, to consolidate and build up European associates and shops, before trying again in the USA. This change is evident in two letters, written four years apart but heralding a real change in emphasis from the casual note of a mainly social visit to something much more serious:

23 October 1969 [to Evangeline Bruce in New York]

Right at this minute I am busily engaged on my third book 'David Hicks on Bathrooms' but leave at the crack of dawn to go and shoot partridge in Spain with Robert de Balkany and on the way back consult Phyllis de Fleurs, Didi Abreu and others on their problems in Paris.

And then:

10 May 1973 [to Mark Hampton, also in New York]

I am moving my office to 43 Conduit Street. I have a very smart red tweed box superimposed in the middle of the brown showroom. The advantages I think will be enormous. A model village is to be constructed at Britwell, and foundations will shortly be laid for my Octagon House. We have got some very chic new fabrics which will remain exclusive to the David Hicks Associates…

I was in the new Paris shop yesterday and was stunned by the quality of the workmanship, boiserie in rough, natural blond wood planks, set against midnight blue lacquer. 'Connaissance des Arts' spent three days photographing the Long Room, and 'La Maison Marie Claire' and 'Architektur und Wohnung' are to photograph next week. I am going down to stay at Le Clos Fiorentina at the end of May to work on Count Cicogna's flat in Monte Carlo, to buy baskets in Avignon and to inspect the Tapis de Cogolin carpet collection. We are all driving down in the Rolls…

The characteristically showing-off letter to Mark, who was just then setting up on his own in New York but was still (in theory, at least) an associate ready to benefit from the new fabrics, is one of so many the two men exchanged over the years that they will always seem to me, above all else, penpals. As the years went by, the showing off came more and more from Mark, but he always tempered his words with the respect of a loyal friend who had once been an assistant, and rather understated his presidential and other grand work. Very sadly, Mark himself died just weeks after my father, so he was unable to give the eulogy at my father's London memorial service, as he had been asked to.

The point of the letter, however, is my father's relationship not with Mark, but with Europe. In 1969, it was partridge taking him on a flying visit to Spain, and his friend Robert de Balkany, married to Princess Maria-Gabriella di Savoia, and he rationalized the trip by a quick stopover in Paris in order to help my godmother, Phyllis Field (now Comtesse de Fleurs), with her apartment. In 1973, he was motoring slowly and in style through France in the Rolls-Royce, looking at French baskets, French carpets and

French jobs, with French and German magazines photographing at Britwell just before. He had, of course, owned a house in France for seven years, and was just about to find a new one.

Associates

My father had had a Swiss associate since the late 1960s, a charming lady decorator named Fleur Vulliod who had written to him out of the blue after seeing yet more pictures of Britwell in *Connaissance des Arts*, asking if there was any chance of collaborating on jobs in Switzerland. Fleur had a charming all-white house in Rolle, above Lake Geneva, and a small shop, which she now renamed David Hicks Suisse. With the huge publicity that every project obtained – together with the strong, definite style, the books that expressed it so well, and the increasing number of products, carpets and fabrics available to them – it was an ideal relationship.

The local associate would do all of the execution of projects, having (in most cases) an initial visit by DH to meet the client, see the property and, in his inimitable style, improvise an agreed design then and there, moving rapidly through the rooms as outlined in his letter to the American quoted earlier (see the chapter on New York). There followed the long, arduous task of carrying out the work, entirely done by the local associate with support from London, where needed, for making special colourways of fabrics, perhaps, or sourcing an upholsterers' braid or light fitting available only from there. Then came the return visit, on which my father was of course bowled over by the quality of the workmanship, the cleverness of the associate's dealing with every little detail, and by his own genius at coming up with the inspired scheme in the first place.

The associate system worked beautifully, especially when the jobs were published in magazines and in his books as David Hicks jobs, with only a minor credit for the local associate. Generally, the associate was less interested in credit, more in making a good business, and was delighted to be in the position of interpreting the master's concept. It was like selling a work of art to a client, organizing its shipment, framing, hanging and other particulars – even an initial visit by the artist to see the place where it was to hang – and sharing with the client the appreciation of the work itself, while enjoying the proceeds of the sale.

All of this was helped, to an extent, by my father and mother's social and family connections. Even if the Paris associates, Barbara Wirth and Christian Badin, were close cousins of famed couturier Hubert de Givenchy, and knew everyone in Paris society, it still helped the partnership to have Lord Mountbatten attend the opening of the small shop in Rue de Tournon, along with a raft of his émigré royal cousins, and have a grand dinner given afterwards at the British Embassy. My father's letters to all of these associates invariably mention some royal outing or other, keeping them all on tenterhooks, as if for the next episode of a very grand soap opera.

Many of the associates over the years were very good designers in their own right – particularly Christian Badin, whose work my father always admired and whose great culture and knowledge was a source of much enjoyment. He liked nothing more than a quick visit to Paris to see what clever new decor Christian had conjured up in the shop, followed by a very good lunch and then a visit to some obscure and delightful fragment of *ancien régime* France. He was given some new little toy by Christian every year for his birthday, his favourite being a sophisticated, Neoclassical-looking candlestick of blond wood. When my sister Edwina was of that age when nice English girls are dispatched to Paris for a little polish, she worked in the shop, reinforcing the family atmosphere.

A typically chic invitation for the opening of David Hicks France.

Room-set at David Hicks Belgium, Brussels, 1976, with Hicks fabrics, carpet, furniture, accessories…

Another room-setting at David Hicks France, designed with customary skill by Christian Badin, 1980.

A view of the Acropolis – from the client's washbasin.

The Athens dining room, dominated by this huge Dali Crucifixion, 1972.

My father designed both his own dinner jacket and my mother's hairstyle, here at its sculptural best, London, 1973.

I went with my parents to visit Christian and his charming mother, who had given her young Givenchy nephew a home during the War and was, in return, given a floor of his wonderful, enormous house. My father admired all of the decoration very much, and loved the detail of the tiny, painted steps that were provided for Mme Badin – who was very old and very small indeed – to ascend to both her bed and her bath. The quirky joys of Anglo-French relationships were not absent from this one, but both French partners remained close friends of my father's until his death, and David Hicks France (now in the capable hands of Marie-Dominique Cunaud) goes from strength to strength.

A View of the Acropolis

There were other jobs, both in Europe and further afield, where no associate was involved, and where my father would collaborate as best he could with a local architect who had often already started construction of a plan that was frequently difficult to furnish. For one Greek shipowner, who had already had his New York apartment transformed back in 1969, he created a stunning penthouse in Athens in an unattractive, modern building that presented a real challenge. The local architect had already started on some 'Classical' detailing that was unfortunately more 1970s than either Classical or Neoclassical Greek – disappointing in the context of the abundance of both styles in the centre of Athens.

It was a challenge, however, and nothing stimulates like a challenge. The view of the Acropolis was extraordinary; the collection of ancient pieces and of Salvador Dali paintings, including a vast Crucifixion and a small portrait of the client, were good material to work with; and the client himself was a marvellous character, whom my father liked enormously. The resulting apartment is one of the best things he ever did, with its

stainless-steel entrance lobby with a niche holding a beautiful ancient statue, the white marble crisp against the immaculate steel. The living room was left as one huge space, and divided by veil-like curtains of chrome beads into dining and living areas, with the client's own desk right in the centre.

The leather-clad desk was straight out of James Bond, with control panels that slid out and presented an array of buttons to adjust everything, from the TV built into the wall to lights, curtains and air conditioning. This very successful Athenian job was typical of a lot of my father's work at the time, with or without an associate in place. Most of the work was executed by the local architect, whose plans were amended by my father, who was responsible for carrying out the design. Many of the tables, and the chrome-and-leather desk that so fascinated me, were made locally from my father's designs, as were a lot of crucial accessories, such as small marble bases for the collection of bronzes. Those pieces that could not be made locally, like Perspex cases, were sent from England, as was the Hicks fabric and the Cogolin rugs from France.

The Empire Grows

A third associate, Nicole Cooremans, opened David Hicks Belgium in Brussels, which was very successful and led to a number of interesting design projects. All of these shops and associates had been greatly helped by my father's chief designer in those years. André Louw was a very gifted, young South African who not only ran the design side of the business under my father but also became a close friend of the whole family, including us children, who all adored him. He was instrumental in setting up a lot of the shops and, when he decided to move back to Johannesburg in 1974, he opened David Hicks South Africa. This was one of the smartest of all the shops, and featured the largest 'H' logo ever made, a huge thing in

bronze-coloured, rough glass mounted on the outside of the shop that dwarfed my father when he was photographed in front of it.

The 'empire' kept on growing. A Munich decorator opened a shop there, with a party attended by the full cast of my grandfather's German cousins. David Hicks Norway was opened by a lady decorator named Gri Moland in Oslo. Nigar Khan, the daughter of a Pakistani admiral, who had worked in the Jermyn Street shop, returned to Karachi and opened a David Hicks shop there. Then Nicola Pagan, who had also worked in London and whose parents were my father's oldest and dearest friends in Australia (and for whom he had decorated two houses there and also the New South Wales Agent General's Office in London), started an associate business in Australia with a leading architectural firm.

My father, of course, delighted in this apparent global expansion, revelling in every new opening, thrilling to the sight of every new corporate letterhead with the increasing number of locations listed at the base. In reality it was merely a number of small, independent decorating shops paying a licence fee to use the name, selling small quantities of his fabrics and carpets, mostly producing little in the way of consultancy work for him, few real design projects. It did, however, feel like a big, multinational concern, and that was the important thing. The company name kept growing, too, and soon became David Hicks International Marketing, the name describing the business.

One project that was a complete joy from beginning to end, and one of the best things of this period, was the work he did at Baronscourt, the Duke of Abercorn's immense, Neoclassical house in Ireland. The Duke was making over the central part of the house to his son, who was married to a beautiful young cousin of my mother's, and my father threw himself into making this into a home for the young family that was comfortable, practical and

stylish. He persuaded them to open up the Long Gallery, which had been turned into three rooms, restoring it to its former glory and revealing all the wonderful, Neoclassical Vitruvius Morrison plasterwork. Our two families became the best of friends, and we would go for long visits to them, driving over from my grandfather's castle.

My father would trawl through the countless cellars and attics, finding treasures of every description heaped up under dust sheets, pulling out chairs, engravings, Victorian cachepots – anything that caught his fancy and that he could use. The house came gradually to life, and it was a revelation to anyone who has known a grim, slightly decrepit, grand Irish house to see this huge place gradually come into bloom. The greatest success for the clients was the family room, created in what had been the ballroom, which they had thought was unusable until my father brightly suggested making an all-in-one modern living room, kitchen, sitting room by building free-standing kitchen units within the space. The family live in this when they are alone, and still love it.

Later On

So far as my father's main design work was concerned, from now on large commercial projects were the thing, with only the occasional private job accepted. Anything smaller than a medium-sized palace in Arabia was frowned upon. (Baronscourt was a rare exception.) The defining moment was the securing of the contract to fit out the interior of the largest private yacht in the world, an Arabian behemoth of a horror that was scarcely to be believed. The work was depressing in the extreme, and it was only the constant hope of huge financial rewards at the end of it all that kept my poor father at it.

He would fly out to the Gulf, an assistant carrying six vast, leather-bound albums of presentation drawings, glossy, slick perspectives of swimming pools that converted

Nicole Cooremans' desk, with a pale wood top on a clear Perspex base, David Hicks Belgium, 1978.

André Louw, chief designer at David Hicks, in the staircase hall at Britwell, 1973.

My father photographed outside André's new David Hicks shop in Johannesburg, South Africa, 1975.

Baronscourt, the family room, with Hicks kitchen islands in emerald-green stained pine breaking up the space, 1976.

My father showing Nahid Ghani where her new sunken rose garden will be built, Vila Verde, Portugal, 1985.

Vila Verde in construction, all three porticoes complete, seen from the cottage ornée, Portugal, 1985.

into discotheques, dining rooms for sixty, guest suites that were more Las Vegas than David Hicks. They would wait days for an audience, only to be told that the albums could not possibly be shown since the 'H' logo so expensively stamped in gold leaf on the covers formed, to an instructed Islamic eye, a Christian cross. Back they flew to London, where new covers were made with less offensive motifs, and they returned to wait another day in alcohol-free, distraction-free, air-conditioned discomfort for another audience.

The last great project of his life was the building of Vila Verde in the Algarve in southern Portugal. Here Amin and Nahid Ghani, delightful Persian clients (my father loathed the modern term Iranian) for whom he had decorated a very sophisticated apartment in London, owned an indifferent holiday house on a golf course, to which they invited our whole family for a week's holiday in 1981. The very first morning, our hostess noticed my father's long face at breakfast and asked him, 'David, I think you don't like my house?', to which he, brutally honest as always, admitted that he did not, and went into some detail as to what exactly was wrong with it. Nahid was horrified, but brightened when he suggested to her that they use the week profitably, to find a site on which to build her a magnificent new house that would be his finest work.

By the time we returned to London, they had settled on a wonderful piece of land with good trees and a distant view of the blue Atlantic. My father, typically, had sat up late every night, sketching dream houses of the Palladian persuasion, his pen outlining first one, then two, and finally three giant classical porticoes on the great house that would be his *chef-d'oeuvre*. They built a small, Regency-style, shell-decorated '*cottage ornée*' at the other edge of the site, to live in while construction was going on, and for my father to come and stay in, looking across to where foundations were already being laid. Nahid and he

travelled extensively, looking at Palladio houses in Italy, Palladian in Ireland and England, at Moghul gardens in India and colonial houses in South Africa, getting inspiration for their dream project.

The completed house was a great success. It had none of the youthful excitement of his early work, but all of his mature, established style of the time. It abounds with tough, 1720s English classical detailing, all executed in plaster by local workers, whom my father thoroughly enjoyed training. The central Great Room is vast, double-height, with a towering George II chimneypiece and huge plaster casts of ancient Persian friezes set into the walls. When the house was finished, it was rather empty, since the contents of the Ghanis' old homes scarcely filled two rooms of this new one, and my father happily lent his friends and clients a lot of old family things – many from Ireland, many originally from his family – which all finished it off perfectly and made him feel very much at home.

He certainly did feel at home. His own bedroom was on the ground floor of the house, wonderfully cool, with a floor of polished terrazzo with big stones on a brown ground, copied from one he had seen in Venice. In it he placed only his own things, including a bed and a rug from Britwell, the Poterie d'Apt chimneypiece from Roquebrune, and the *Directoire* engravings that he had bought in Avignon that first summer. He made two collages specially for the room, framed in Perspex boxes, old pictures of his long-lost, adored brother John mounted on his hunter, little David on his pony. The writing paper he designed for the house was based on his grandfather's 1900 paper. Surrounded by things from his childhood, in this splendid house that he had created, he was very happy. He made a beautiful and elaborate garden, and had the good fortune to find that Amin Ghani was as dedicated and enthusiastic a gardener as he was himself. All was perfection.

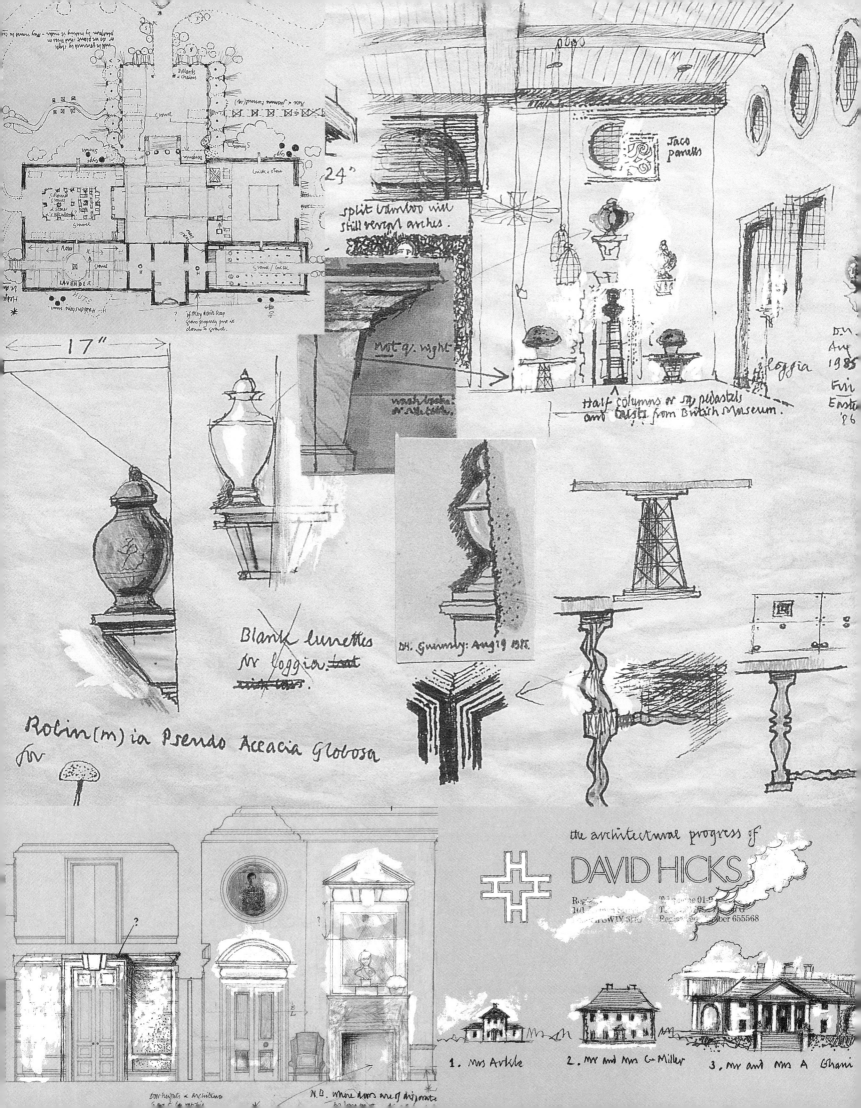

the architectural progress of

DAVID HICKS

1. Mrs Arkile   2. Mr and Mrs C. Miller   3. Mr and Mrs A. Ghani

CHAPTER NINE: Living with Design

David Hicks: Living with Design was published in 1979. It was dedicated 'To my father-in-law and in memory of my mother-in-law with affection and admiration'. The book was designed, once again, by Nick Jenkins and had long features on Britwell (which we had just sold); on Baronscourt; and on my grandfather's Classiebawn Castle, which had recently been purged of its eau de nil and black 1950s severity in a complete redecoration by my father that also, sadly, removed much of its atmosphere and charm. My grandfather did not live to see the book, being murdered by the IRA on his beloved fishing boat while we were all staying with him at Classiebawn on 27 August.

For me, it was the end of my childhood, since I had just turned 16 and the bright sun, around which my childhood world had always revolved, was suddenly and brutally taken away. With my grandfather were killed a young Irish boy who helped on the boat, my uncle's aged mother and one of his twin sons, with whom I had always been particularly close. My own loss did not compare to my cousins' or my mother's, but it was devastating to us all. It was a very strange time, as we all tried to put as brave a face on events as we could, marching without tears in my grandfather's huge, ceremonial funeral procession to Westminster Abbey, going back to our lives in the shadow of this very public bereavement.

My father, having relocated the business to Jermyn Street, had also moved from our Chelsea apartment to a set of rooms in Albany, just across Piccadilly, where he had longed to live since decorating a similar set for a client in the 1950s. This became his London home for twenty years, until he died. My mother still lives there. Albany was so much to his taste that it is hard now to imagine him anywhere else in town. Everything about it suited him: the hushed quiet in the centre of that bustling city, the severe Englishness of the whole place, and the beauty of Henry Holland's twin ranges of stuccoed apartments along the Ropewalk. This, named after the similar structures used in boatyards for winding ropes, was a walk covered with a long, hipped, Chinese-looking roof, leading from the mansion, old Melbourne House, on its courtyard off Piccadilly, to the back door on to Burlington Gardens.

Against this severe, slightly bleak background, he could flourish – with a uniformed porter in the lodge at the front ready to announce and guide visitors, with that intimidating, slightly unnerving, long walk to his staircase, the chilly, grey stone stair with its hard, metal railings, and finally the large, round brass doorbell. The whole context had the anonymity of a traditional English suit, which my father soon began to order in quantity from Messrs Huntsman, conveniently near his new back door. The apartments are all identical, having been built as gentlemens' lodgings in 1802, one better than staying at your St James's club but with none of the complication of a whole house: two good-sized rooms with fireplaces for sitting and sleeping, a small hallway and a back room for a servant, a boxroom in the attic and a bit of a cellar for wine and coal. What more does one need?

My father was delighted with his 'set', as the snobbish Albany parlance describes the apartments, or sets of chambers. (The building, by the way, must never be called The Albany, or Albany House, or any other dreadful, class-revealing misnomer.) This kind of snobbery thrilled its newest resident, who thoroughly enjoyed his twenty years of correcting anyone poorly educated enough to use the wrong words. He resolved to make the rooms in the spirit of the time they were built, and set to work on a modern version of 1840, centring the scheme on a large and immensely grand bed that he draped '*a la Polonais*' and covered with the remaining scarlet silk damask that he had had woven specially, eighteen years before, for our dining room at Britwell. The bed, described theatrically as 'a bed to receive one's doctors from, a bed to die in', was placed centrally in the second room, seen through the wide opening from the living room, which it dominated entirely.

He had always had elaborate fantasies about splendid beds, the result of too many uncomfortable nights as a wartime child, a reluctant soldier and an impoverished art student, coupled with a fascination for luxury glimpsed on house and museum visits, and in magazines and books. As a young man he was utterly bewitched by a framed print of one of James Pryde's strange, dark 1920s paintings of dramatic, high beds with Baroque curtains and moody lighting. Literary excursions into Firbank, Mitford, Waugh and the letters of Lord Chesterfield only increased his obsessive fascination with superior sleeping arrangements. His favourite fictional moment was when Lord Marchmain, returning from Venetian exile to die at Brideshead, settles himself into the old state bed in one of the huge rooms on the ground floor of the great house.

Albany Once More

Albany lasted in this guise for sixteen years, until my father decided that enough was enough, and he simply had to redecorate completely. This was after a series of disasters with his business, which by the end had borne his name but made him effectively its hostage, forced to approve of bad commercial interiors that he loathed but had to give his signature to. More and more he had looked elsewhere for a vent for his bubbling creativity – to garden design especially, and to creating a collection of jewellery. When the company finally went bust, he was immensely relieved and, anticipating an entire new career, threw himself into remaking Albany with the same gusto he had shown forty years before.

The design had something of his early style about it, too, with its severe, Vandyke brown walls, masses of white paint and spare furnishing. Wanting more space, he removed the kitchen, building instead two small cupboards in the now much larger hall. One held a tiny fridge, and the other housed a small microwave and an electric kettle. Since the only cooking that either of my parents ever did was to boil an egg, this was no great blow, although my mother does find it rather awkward removing her boiled egg from the kettle. She was permitted to see the transformed set only when it was entirely finished, and went into rhapsodies of praise at his genius in making the hall seem so large, before she realized that the kitchen had actually disappeared.

He described it to me:

I love it because it's so wonderfully simple and refined and there's nothing to worry about. I love not seeing the neighbours. It's frightfully important never, ever to see them, and particularly not to see their badly glazed, plate-glass windows. They, of course, look at my beautiful 18th century astragals. I don't want to know about the outside world. I don't like today at all. So this suits me very well.

I wanted to make a statement that was fresh and different and new, with no bloody floral chintzes, something that didn't need flowers in order to be photographed. There's a strong message, saying 'Hicks is still alive and vital, doing something completely new and different.' If you look at it in a magazine, and you look at other bits of the magazine, of any nationality, it always stands out as being totally, totally original, whereas all the other ones are full of nonsense or just too pretty.

There is a comfortable sofa for your mother to sit on and read her book. She doesn't feel very

Albany, the first version, with 'a bed to die in' – shiny scarlet glazed cotton on the outside, scarlet silk damask within.

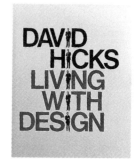

Living with Design, 1979. The 'I's are tiny pictures of the author, posing elegantly with a cigarette.

Garden Design, 1981. Almost entirely in black and white, the twelve colour pages were of completely green gardens.

In the garden at The Grove, a portrait relief of Edwina Mountbatten surrounded by shells she found in Tahiti.

Hicks the countryman, in his gardening clothes and leaning against a stone urn at The Grove, 1982.

comfortable here, but then Albany's not a place for women.

Sadly, it was really much too late to restart his career in any meaningful way, which he had hoped the publicity of the new Albany might achieve. He did do some new designing, including two houses in Michigan. There was also one last client in London who, having explained that the unsightly white plastic object on her wall was part of the burglar alarm, was told that she might as well get rid of it and the alarm, since she had absolutely nothing worth stealing. She fell in love with him at once, utterly seduced by his bizarre mixture of rudeness and charm, and was still smitten when he died, leaving her house half-complete.

Albany, in both of its creations, was a far cry from one of his first homes in London, from which he had written to his mother, 'I have taken a big room on the ground floor in Chester Street. There is a monkey in the basement and rather a strong smell of stale fish in the hall, but the landlady is nice and it's a jolly nice room and as it's on the ground floor there are no beastly stairs!'

The Grove

The last years of my father's life were dominated by his comfortable life with my mother in their new house in the country, The Grove, a mile from Britwell. They had sold the big house in 1978 but kept most of the land, so my mother continued to ride her horse as before, and my father carried on planting thousands of trees every year and became increasingly more of a countryman. He travelled just as much as he ever had and, if he was frustrated at times by not being the centre of a design empire any longer, he had the satisfaction, at least, of universal recognition of what he had achieved over his long career. As more and more magazines and books appeared crediting him with inventing geometric carpets, with having revolutionized English postwar decorating or with having established interior design as a profession in the UK, he reflected on his new status:

British Airways Club World, 28th March '94

At the end of the day all that matters is what I have achieved. Not at all bad. I am suddenly being built up everywhere as the Grand Old Man of interior design. I have become a hero in my own lifetime. It never ceases to amaze me what an effect I can have on people. Why? But I do. It is rather an asset. They say I am King! I must live on. 'A living legend'!

It would be lovely to be rich – I fear I never will be but occasionally I reach out in extravagance. I love life and specially work & achievement and I would like to live until I am uncomfortable – around 75–78? There is still so much that I have not been allowed to do.

He died five years and a day later. The Grove had been their home since he wrote to me in March 1980:

I sit at my desk in the library, for the first time, to write to you. All the packing cases are gone, the hall is now clear, though not yet clean. The library floor is painted, so is the chimney breast, awaiting my grandmother's old silk velvet evening skirt. Lord Shaftesbury is hung and lit over the chimney and looks most content. I have the Turkey carpet down and Granny's two wing chairs – one from your old bedroom in khaki and scarlet still – perhaps I'll keep it like that. My bed canopy is hung. In the 18th century they referred to that sort of bed as a 'standing bed'!

More and more he revelled in reminiscence, in old descriptions, antique terminology, obscure old recipes.

One of his favourite occupations was to find particularly strange puddings and pies in his grandmother's Victorian cookbook and then torment his cook with complaints about the consistency of the sauce when she had been struggling to replicate the hundred-year-old recipe. He attempted to form a lake in a low-lying field away from the house, and was determined to use only the proper eighteenth-century technique of puggling. Somehow he located an expert puggling man, who organized the delivery of the requisite flock of sheep, whose busy, fenced-in feet puggled away for days, trampling the clay floor of the 'lake' into what should have been a waterproof lining. The lake was not a success, and the resulting small pond was immediately screened from view by the planting of several thousand trees right up to its edge.

His Last Room

My father rearranged his bedroom memorabilia cabinets a few months before his death. One of the chief features of what he did at The Grove was to make liberal use of a refined and delicate 'Gothick' in new windows and glazed doors, which he continued in his bedroom with the pair of glazed cabinets with ogee-arched doors. The cabinets held memorabilia right from the beginning, for no one loved objects or precious old things more than he did. Typically clever detailing went into the lighting, with simple light bulbs concealed by little Gothic shapes cut from plywood and added to the panes. He had rearranged the whole room a couple of years before his death, moving the bed from its old position between the glazed cabinets, and facing the window, to the end wall facing the door. After eighteen years, this was a sudden change. Now, when you entered the room, you faced the bed, while he – from below its small canopy, from under the soft, fur bedspread – could look sideways through the window and out to his beloved garden.

The garden was his greatest creation, his most complete work, and he had dwelt on its plans for long evenings at his library desk. In it he had struggled physically day after day for nineteen years, returning to the house with hands often bloodied from another intense bout of pruning his adored roses, those impressively titled ladies whom he loved to introduce to his many garden visitors. 'Lady Hillingdon, Mme Isaac Pereire…,' he would grandly announce to startled garden club members from Nottingham or Buenos Aires. He had designed the garden around the views from the principal rooms of the house, among which his own bedroom was not included. The south garden is therefore seen only obliquely from his bedroom window, being centred on the tall Regency window of the adjacent drawing room.

The composition is formed by lines of severely clipped hornbeam trees, with hedges beneath that form green walls against which the trees' trunks stand as columns. These handsome blocks of green architecture frame an improvised opening in the ancient farm wall of soft, red brick, beyond which successive lines of beech hedge and chestnut trees stretch to the horizon. From my father's bedroom window, the sideways view has none of the formality of the drawing room's proscenium-like view. Here, instead, the eye slides diagonally across carefully marshalled rectangles of box and immaculate lawn, over the trees' perfectly smooth tops, through the brick opening and out into the open fields beyond. The land rises up away from the house, the horizon always comfortingly high, the garden like a fragile cup holding the house and the life within it.

It has a modest half-tester, a canopy that matches the small, intimate scale of the room. Ever one to tinker and improvise, my father had the local carpenter dismantle his grandfather's Regency wardrobe, using its anthemion-carved mahogany frieze as a pelmet for the bed curtains.

Out shooting with his new whiskers, 1991, adapted by him from an old print of a Victorian Highland soldier.

My father's 1990 sketch for his drawing studio at The Grove, where he later lay in a coffin of his own design.

Sketch for a new house in the Algarve, Portugal, 1994. After the success of Vila Verde, my father longed to build more.

The memorabilia cabinets: the Mountbatten side, 1998.

Edwina Mountbatten, 'the most charismatic woman…'

The tsarevitch's lifebelt, and a watercolour by his sister Olga.

My grandfather with Russian cousins and his Aunt Ella, Grand Duchess Serge, 1912.

The drawer-base of the wardrobe went elsewhere, while the body of it was used here for his few clothes, with a plywood top that he himself covered with marbleized paper found in Venice. On it stood a notice in his large, elaborate italic hand: 'Do NOT dust. DH'. The small room combines bed and bath, with the bath placed in an alcove between two little corner cupboards with panelled doors. One of these holds the loo, a tiny space filled with books and Victorian sewing things of his grandmother's.

In the window is the washbasin, uncomfortably low in order not to block the lovely view, set into one of five bookcases that crowd the small space. The books are all white, off-white, cream or ivory – many are old vellum bindings that slowly lightened over the years as long nights of insomnia, together with the proximity of water and soap, prompted feverish sessions of book-washing. On the walls hang eighteenth-century architectural drawings, while the low bookcases are dotted with Chinese agate, rock-crystal and quartz scholars' rocks and bowls, also eighteenth-century. Beside the bath stand two mildly Gothic English hall chairs.

The signs that the room was actually lived in were never easy to spot: a single piece of soap in a bowl by the washbasin, or a small notepad and pen by the bed. Some false books by the window hinged open to reveal toothbrush and shaving things. Towels hung inside the little loo in the corner. It was monastic in feeling, a space of great contemplation, crowded in a way, but hugely spare in another. This was a room in which bodily comfort and ease were ruled by a higher, aesthetic principle. The personal life was expressed not through the detritus of the lives of us lesser mortals, none of our dog-eared paperbacks, family pictures, telephones, magazines… Here, instead, the life was memorialized, with the two glazed memorabilia cabinets arranged with the thoroughness and sensibility of a small Victorian museum.

The Demise of David Hicks

One cabinet holds Mountbatten things; the other, Hicks. The Mountbatten cabinet is nearer the bed – pragmatic as ever, he kept the prettier and more glamorous side of his life nearer than the relics of his Essex upbringing. Closest to the bed, he placed things from my mother's family and childhood, from pictures of her with Nehru in India, or riding at Broadlands, to a toy lifebelt made by the tsarevitch's sailor servant, framing a watercolour of the Russian fleet escorting the imperial yacht, *Standart*. Sir Ernest Cassel's silk-embroidered monogram, carefully picked off his Edwardian linen sheets, sits next to a glamorous 1920s studio photograph of his granddaughter, my grandmother, Edwina Mountbatten. Luggage labels, matchbooks and old medals mix theatrically with pasted-on background pictures of jewels torn from magazines.

By the door, meanwhile, the Hicks cabinet holds assorted old things from his own family: lorgnettes, tartan purses, eighteenth-century cross-written letters, his father's Masonic jewels, pictures of his brother John Hicks on his hunter before the War, and charming cut-out, hand-coloured seaside photographs, relics of an idyllic, untroubled childhood brought rudely to a close. Mixed with these are fragments from his career: David Hicks signs and cards, tiny fabric swatches, a tile, a row of eggs painted by Mark Hampton with views of Britwell and given as Easter presents every year.

A few months before he died, my father summoned me to his library, where he always sat at Sir Ernest Cassel's massive, mahogany partner's desk with the self-conscious gravity of some menacing headmaster half-remembered from his own schooldays. He had photographed every inch of the newly arranged cabinets, and written captions on the pictures, detailing the provenance, date and significance of every object. 'You won't remember, otherwise,' he explained. 'I'll be dead soon, and no one will have a clue. Not after I'm gone.' The pictures were carefully placed in a drawer. Two weeks before he died, I went with our daughter Ambrosia (then barely a year old) to say 'Good morning' to her grandfather, whom we found happily stretched out in his bathtub, luxuriously soaking on a Sunday morning. Ambrosia looked with the bright and curious eyes of youth at his withered old body under the water and kissed him without a tinge of awkwardness.

On the afternoon of 29 March 1998, four days after his 69th birthday – 'in my 70th year', as he would say – my father died in his bed, his eyes gazing out at the sky, where plump clouds were scudding across his beloved garden. I had been reading to him from a volume of royal memoirs, from which I recall a description of the gravel outside old Montagu House being raked every day, whether it had been driven on or not. My mother had found something about him in that day's Sunday paper and she read that to him, telling him, 'You see, no one's forgotten you. You're still as famous as ever.' He smiled with pleasure at both readings, but not as much as when our charming, gentle priest, Martin Garner, arrived to say prayers for him, and we all knelt at the foot of his bed in a scene so perfectly romantic and pictorial that finally, yes, all was complete: he could leave us.

His funeral was arranged entirely according to his directions, which he had written out carefully by hand in a small parchment-covered book, inscribed on spine and cover with 'The Demise of David Hicks' and left conveniently in the bookcase next to his bed. He had laboured over these instructions for several years, edited and re-edited the orders of service for both country funeral and London memorial service, Tippexing out the names of ushers or readers who predeceased him. His obituaries were fulsome, and soon the newspapers caught on to his last project, his hand reaching out from beyond to design his own funeral. He who loved his press more

than anything then had the immortal distinction of a leader in the *Daily Telegraph* on the subject of 'designer funerals'.

Time magazine's obituary called him the '60's avatar of interior design...a sworn enemy of chintz, eschewed the staid flowery prints in favor of eye-popping solids, which he boldly mingled with modern paintings and patterned carpets.' The very first of his geometric fabrics, 'Daisy Daisy', a pattern of round wheel motifs adapted from Egyptian wall decorations, was also the last, having been used in his redecoration of Albany, and then by me as a lining for his handsome coffin, which was made to his design in grey-stained sycamore with (as per his instructions) 'No handles', which he had thought 'frightfully common'. He lay very grandly in state in his pavilion in the garden, as he had intended, his coffin open, dressed elegantly with a David Hicks tie and his pockets stuffed with obituaries and press cuttings (as my mother said, 'He'll need something good to read where he's going').

He was borne across the pavilion's little drawbridge with some difficulty, and then his gardeners and I carried him on to the ivy-strewn trailer of his Range Rover – with his flag up for the last time – which took him to pretty Ewelme church for the funeral. Afterwards, in a snaking, winding procession of cars (for a huge crowd had turned up to see him off), we took him back from Ewelme, along the drives of The Grove, the master leading a tour of his garden one last time, to Brightwell Baldwin, where he now lies, at peace, in the shadow of the church. Afterwards the crowd of mourners came back to the house for a drink and a sandwich. I took a few of them up to see his room, just as he had left it, and to admire the memorabilia cabinets. One, a talented designer who had worked closely with him for many years, asked me with tears in his eyes how anyone would believe that a man could have lived and died in that room, which was so beautiful but showed so little sign of life…

The Hicks side: Nixon, and a watercolour by Iris Hicks.

Mark Hampton's painted Easter eggs of Britwell views.

Little David on the beach, and some Salters' memorabilia.

More of my father's family things, kept in the cabinet furthest from his bed.

There were only two things in my father's life that he did not design. The first was his logo, his symbol, his 'H' sign. This he put on everything – on houses and cars, on writing paper, on sheets, carpets, fabrics, notepads, towels, on scarlet-heeled men's evening shoes, on tacky Japanese jewellery – everywhere, in fact, that he could. He stopped short of planting it in a box parterre outside The Grove drawing-room window, but only when he had done a very realistic sketch of it full-grown and doubtless thought it just a little exaggerated. The logo was designed for him (one of three alternatives) as a thankyou, by a young would-be designer named Richard Pullen, for whom he had found a job in Terence Conran's office.

The 'H' logo fascinated me as a child, partly perhaps because I slept, from the age of 7, in J. P. Stevens sheets with a repeat pattern of 'H' logos and squares. I would spend hours at school making new geometric patterns using the 'H' logo, carefully drawing them out in Indian ink on squared paper and sending them with great pride to my father. This book is covered in a version of the original sheeting design, which seems especially apt, in that I spent much of my childhood enveloped in that design, and now my own small tribute to my father's memory is in turn wrapped in it.

The second thing that he did not design was his gravestone. That he left to me. He had tried a couple of sketches of miniature pyramids, but they looked too dolls'-house-like, too fussy, and in the end he told me that I would have to do it. I was intimidated by this task, but set to it when my mother grew impatient to see the thing finished. I took the form of an eighteenth-century Gothic pinnacle atop the Brightwell Baldwin church tower that looms over his grave, stripped it of its crockets, and had this cut from his favourite English stone, fossil-rich Purbeck from Dorset. On the slightly pyramidal top I had chiselled the form of his 'H' logo, as if one of his *David Hicks on...*

book covers had been laid on to it, exactly the same size as on the original books.

The finished stone was charmingly described by my father's great friend and church companion, Christopher Gibbs, who had given the eulogy at his Ewelme funeral, as 'an obelisk in bud'. This delighted me, since there was nothing that my father had liked more than obelisks, and the thought that something of beauty was growing from where he lay seemed very poetic. It was important for me to have some very direct link to his work on the stone, and nothing was more definitive of his style and his achievement than those early books with their 'H' logos emblazoned on the covers. At the back of my mind was the thought that he had asked me to do a book on his life, a proper biography – something he had always longed for. My initial idea was to republish some of his early books, but I was quickly persuaded to make a new book instead.

Starting to write, I realized that I would be able to do neither an impersonal, objective design commentary nor a serious biography of my father. The first was not possible from me, his son, while the second would not suit the pictures. Instead, I have made a very personal book, a sketch of his career and life, followed by my own selection of some of his best residential work. Since the book centres around pictures of our own houses, and we did not have unlimited space, it seemed logical to limit it to residential work. His commercial interiors (shops, restaurants, offices) were some of his best, but I had to limit the scope somehow, and this seemed the best way. In the text I tried to look at his influences and working methods, but inevitably was unable to refrain from telling stories of my own childhood, my own memories of him. My purpose, however, was not to tell a story, but to publish images – many never seen before – of David Hicks's work, which many people find just as inspiring today as they ever did. Here, then, are those images…

Reportage de Rosamond Bernier

Angleterre

Il y a environ deux ans, Mr. David Hicks et sa femme, Lady Pamela, achetaient à Britwell Salome, petit village de l'Oxford[...] un très joli manoir en briques du XVIIIᵉ siècle. Mr. Hicks est un des plus jeunes et des plus brillants décorateurs de son [...] aussi se demandait-on avec curiosité comment il aménagerait sa demeure. Les photos que nous publions ici renseignen[t...] sujet et mettent en valeur les caractéristiques principales de son style.

La maison est grande et comporte des parties d'une architecture quelque peu solennelle (la salle à manger à colonnes[...] vestibule), le propriétaire a donc cherché avant tout à créer une atmosphère de gaieté. Il aime le blanc et l'associe souven[t...] des couleurs claires et vives. Des cotonnades et d'autres tissus simples servent à garnir des sièges de style Louis XVI pei[nts...] blanc. David Hicks recouvre par endroits le sol de tapis de jute et certaines des fenêtres ont des rideaux de toile écrue d[ont...] bordure est faite des sangles qu'utilisent les tapissiers pour la confection des fauteuils. A Britwell House, on rapproche vol[ontiers...] époques et civilisations différentes; des sculptures primitives et des objets[...] d'Extrême-Orient voisinent avec des céramiques suédoises contemporaines. Avec la somptueuse argenterie que Lady Pamel[a...]

Blenheim
Dichie

n décorateur s'installe

lle, on ne craint pas d'utiliser des coupes danoises en matière plastique d'un beau ton améthyste. Les chambres à coucher
illes de bains, toutes très différentes les unes des autres, sont pourtant toutes traitées d'une façon très personnelle. Les lits
aldaquin, parfois ils donnent simplement l'impression d'en comporter grâce à une draperie suspendue au plafond. Aucune
bains n'a de carreaux de céramique; elles sont installées comme de véritables pièces d'habitation. Leurs sols sont
rts de moquette et les murs ornés de tableaux sont souvent tendus de tissus. Des meubles, des lustres de cristal, des
s de vermeil pour les brosses à dents, le téléphone à côté de la baignoire invitent à y séjourner. Les moindres détails ont
jet de soins minutieux: les armoires des chambres à coucher sont tendues de gaies cotonnades, à chaque fenêtre la
est contrôlée et tamisée par des stores vénitiens, des contre-rideaux transparents blancs à demi tirés et des rideaux.
deux grandes pièces modernes donnant sur la roseraie, David Hicks termine à l'heure actuelle un studio pour sa
ll y réinstallera les panneaux décoratifs faits pour la mère de celle-ci, Lady Edwina Mountbatten, par le peintre anglais
istler dans les années qui précédèrent la guerre.

Wttingham

*ck Bar
Nottingham.*

HOME DECOR Employing an interior
decorator at all is incredibly ROGUE. But if you
must, among the least ROGUE are John Siddeley,
David Hicks and John Fowler. Antique is GO
if borrowed. Aubusson carpets are ABORT.
Owning original paintings is ROGUE, unless
they were inherited when they become ABORT.
The most GO painting to have at the moment is
Goya's Duke of Wellington.

Britwell Salome was bought by my parents in 1960 and was my father's laboratory and showroom for nineteen years. In the beginning the house was left deliberately rather bare, in the manner of the early eighteenth century (when the house was built). Over time this changed and by the end it was so crowded that a Sotheby's house sale, held at Britwell to sell its contents, lasted for three days. The handsome brick façade of pedimented central block and symmetrical wings, and the imposing stone column, suggested the minor architectural glories of the hall, staircase and chapel within, but not the variety of spectacular decorative games played out in them by my father. The following pictures show some – by no means all – of the rooms in what was, as well as our home, the world's largest showroom. Here, a page from his 1963 scrapbook with Britwell in French *L'Oeil* and my grandfather peeping out from underneath, in full evening regalia, after dinner at Britwell before a ball at Blenheim.

OPPOSITE: The hall – its walls painted by my father in a shade of bronze that he discovered beneath sixteen layers of Victorian paint – with the plaster and wood architectural features in a soft, buff stone colour. The floor is traditional limestone and black marble. The furnishing is very spare, with painted hall chairs, an ebony Gothic chair from Horace Walpole's Strawberry Hill and a white-horsehair-covered sofa. The doorway leads to the staircase hall beyond.

BELOW: A detail of the staircase hall, hung with my father's first wallpaper design, adapted from a seventeenth-century Portuguese damask and hand-blocked for him by Coles. Against this, beneath an eighteenth-century portrait group, a typical Hicks tablescape combines Chinese jade, Roman marble souvenirs from the Grand Tour, a Provençal basket filled with fresh potpourri, an English 1720 earthenware jar and a curious black stone finial.

OPPOSITE & ABOVE: The Octagon Room opened on to the drawing room and held a large and very well-stocked drinks table, the telephone and music. My father found the black and gilt Gothic chimney in a shop, only later discovering that it follows a design in his favourite handbook, Batty Langley's *Gothic Architecture* of 1742. Details (above) include a table covered with a tapa (painted barkcloth) made by Queen Salote of Tonga and her ladies as a gift for my mother.

LEFT & ABOVE: Four drawing-room tablescapes, organized by colour, their contents ranging from ancient to new. The blue table combines precious lapis lazuli objects with a lighter, and a translucent plastic maquette for a Rory McEwen sculpture. The pink blossom enlivens a mass of Chinese rock crystal and small gold boxes on a white marble-topped gueridon.

OPPOSITE: A woven oatmeal cotton covers the drawing-room walls, against which hung only modern, abstract paintings. The carpet was made to a Hicks design at Cogolin, while the sofas are covered in one of his first, small-repeat geometric fabrics. Early Wedgwood adds to the room's fresh look.

OPPOSITE: At one end of the drawing room, an eighteenth-century Irish carved table, originally heavy and dark, was painted white and given a new top of porphyry, my father's favourite stone since his visit to Egypt. On this he arranged a whole collection of porphyry objects – some ancient, some barely antique – together with a basalt fragment of a pharaoh's head on a clear Perspex block and a group of red-leather scroll-boxes.

BELOW: The library, where my father worked at Sir Ernest Cassel's old desk, with Cassel's red-leather cushion from his car on a black felt-covered armchair. The walls were covered with black paper, against which the aluminium uprights of the simple kitchen shelving gleamed. At the bottom of the righthand bookcase are ranged my father's scrapbooks, with their red-leather labels on black spines.

LEFT & ABOVE: My mother's study was originally painted by Rex Whistler in grisaille, turquoise and silver for my grandmother Edwina Mountbatten in 1937, as her boudoir in her new Park Lane apartment. Removed when the war started, it went to Broadlands for safekeeping (happily, since a bomb in 1941 destroyed the rest of the room, including the ceiling, which was also painted by Whistler). My father reassembled the panels for my mother, keeping the Whistler-painted desk and using other 1930s furniture from the same apartment with a collection of green jade and fresh, white upholstery. Painted above the fireplace is Broadlands, while my grandmother reclines naked with Father Time against the clock.

OPPOSITE & ABOVE: The breakfast room (opposite), where we usually ate, was a low, cosy room and led to the vast splendour of the dining room. The contrast between the two rooms was extreme. Here, all was earthy simplicity, with scrubbed-pine table, oatmeal- and biscuit-coloured fabrics, painted Georgian country chairs and Staffordshire pottery on simple brackets. The dining room (above), on the other hand, was all studied magnificence, opulent gestures of grandeur – from the gold beakers for water and gold boxes of cigarettes, to the huge wing chairs in sumptuous scarlet velvet sitting beside the fire.

ABOVE & OPPOSITE: The oval dining room at Britwell, which was added to the house around 1760 as a private chapel for its Catholic owners, has an elaborate, domed plasterwork ceiling crowded with symbols of the Mass. The Hicks-era deep-claret walls and scarlet silk damask fabric reflect this origin, as does the profusion of magnificent silver from Sir Ernest Cassel's collection. As always, this wealth of intense colour is balanced by a white frame – here the crisp white linen cloth and white-painted sidetables, ceiling and woodwork contrast with the stone-coloured window surrounds. The crystal chandelier follows Hicks rules: real candles, no electricity, and hung as low as possible. On the chimney, beneath the gilded 1720 mirror, a highly figured gilt Rococo cup stands between two *faux*-porphyry cachepots.

LEFT & ABOVE: The two quadrant passages leading to the East Wing, decorated ten years apart. The lower quadrant (left), connecting the staircase hall to the Long Room, was decorated in 1971 with masculine grey walls and fitted coconut doormatting. The Victorian plaster busts of the continents stand on mahogany and ebony bases of Hicks design, flanking portraits of some of my mother's more forgettable ancestors. The upper quadrant (above) was used as a guestroom at first, and here it is decorated in 1964 in High Victorian style with Jaipur cotton on the walls, a Morris design on the bed, Indonesian batiks on the lampshades. The space is crowded with oddments of nineteenth-century furniture and pictures, and what my father always called 'Turkey carpets'.

LEFT & ABOVE: The Long Room, decorated in 1971 as an extra living room, somewhere to have a big party or to sit alone listening to Wagner played at immense volume. Pink felt stuck to the walls, scarlet Hicks 'Chevron' design curtains, purple and red upholstery — all gave a fiery excitement that was somewhat surprising in the green English countryside. The sandstone horse's head was commissioned from a carver in Rajasthan, whom my father found replacing one on a Rajput palace; its base is stainless steel. My grandmother's Giles Grendey scarlet lacquered chairs surround the magenta card table. Sir Ernest Cassel's piano (above top) was given modern Hicks legs and eggshell lacquer, while a tablecloth of African Kente cloth (above) works well with the Hicks geometric carpet.

ABOVE: Two of the Britwell guest rooms. The Indian room (left), decorated in 1962 after my father's first trip to the subcontinent, has everything covered in different-striped cottons bought in India, with a silver peacock in the window, Indian wildlife miniatures and an Indo-Portuguese ivory inlaid cabinet as a bedside table. The Oak Room (right), instead, was an essay in updating Olde England, the Morris bed fabric and traditional rush matting made crisply modern by the off-white beamed ceiling and walls, and plain terracotta wool curtains.

OPPOSITE: My parents' bedroom, with emerald-green-and-white carpet made to a Hicks design by Tai Ping in Hong Kong. The bed, covered in white glazed cotton quilted in the 'H'-logo pattern, was hung with a 'Zed' geometric print, as were the curtains, with shaped pelmets adapted from a seventeenth-century Swedish design. At the foot of the bed is a bottle-green silk velvet stool. The dressing table holds my Mountbatten grandmother's silver-gilt Art Deco dressing set.

ABOVE: My mother had an airy, white bathroom (left), with a central bath, very simple, with little furniture apart from the elaborate 1760 English cabinet and the two red armchairs, designed by Lord Snowdon for the Prince of Wales' investiture in 1967. The carpet for the small downstairs cloakroom (right) was a Hicks design for the Prince, and incorporates his feathers within a geometric pattern. The walls were covered in blue felt.

OPPOSITE: My father's bathroom was his finest expression of disgust at the 'many beautiful houses sadly marred by the drabness, unoriginality or plain discomfort of their bathing arrangements' (*David Hicks on Bathrooms*, 1970). He always tried to place the bath in the middle of the room – rather as a tub would have been placed in an earlier age before the advent of plumbing. Here it is encased in deep moulded panelling, to match the original room, with a stippled granite paint finish. The black felt screen with brass nailing hid the loo.

Madame Rubinstein, at home in a flame silk suit by Balenciaga, arranges lilies for a low table-setting. The Trevedy painting on the wall beside her is one of several unusual works in her fine collection of twentieth-century artists. A larger aspect of her living-room, below, shows walls in purple woven linen which give rich contrast background to the paintings that adorn them. The Belter chairs, with their lacelike carving, are nineteenth-century American, the magenta and purple felt upholstery is modern

Princess Gourielli, known the world over as Helena Rubinstein, is at home to us in her fabulous "little" apartment in Knightsbridge, decorated for her by the brilliant young English designer, David Hicks

Photographed by Peter Tauber

A bedroom for a princess is painted in yellow gold to background an intricately carved sixteenth-century Portuguese bedstead that David Hicks discovered in a small shop in Estoril. The magnificent coverings are in Thai silk. Also in this room, but not shown, are an eighteenth-century English silver table . . . and two water-colours by Chagall

Below, right, the tiny sitting-room on the first floor of the apartment is a quiet retreat with a sky-and-rooftops view. Rich, restful velvet walls make a perfect background for softly muted brocade upholstery in lime and silver-gold. The gilt mirror is seventeenth-century

Sarah Chester Beatty

43

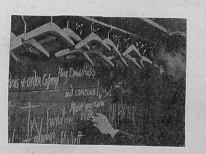

David Hicks first emerged as a designer in London in 1954 with the publication of his own house in South Eaton Place. Helena Rubenstein's London apartment of 1961, seen here together with some curtain sketches in his scrapbook for that year, was a turning point in his career, firmly establishing him as the designer of the moment. On the following pages are a selection of jobs – all private, all in London or the country nearby – beginning with his own house in St Leonard's Terrace in Chelsea. Above all, what unites the interiors on these pages (which date from 1963 to 1978) are the vibrant, exciting colours and the famous geometric carpets and fabrics. To an early client who worried that his wife would be unhappy with my father's 'clashing' scheme of a magenta, vermilion and orange bedroom, he explained: 'Colours do not clash, they vibrate. Your wife will find it exciting.'

OPPOSITE: In the 1960s, in his small London town house in Chelsea, overlooking Wren's Royal Hospital, my father lacquered the walls of the living room in 'Coca-Cola colour', with woodwork and ceiling (as always) sharply defined in white. The sofa had a summer cover, shown here, of white linen – also used, unlined, as curtains. The yellow Ellsworth Kelly painting perfectly matched the hard, graphic mood of the room. A Hicks-designed table of glass and aluminium sat happily with the 1780 chair (signed 'Tilliard') and the Chinese lacquered *étagère*.

ABOVE & RIGHT: On the chimney and on a marble-topped Swedish commode are seemingly artless arrangements of minerals, modern sculpture and some dried grass, with drawings by Graham Sutherland and Keith Vaughn (who had taught my father at the Central School of Art).

DAVID HICKS HOUSE, ST LEONARD'S TERRACE, LONDON

LEFT: This small breakfast room was created around 1970 next to the living room. It was tented and loosely draped in a new Hicks torn-paper floral design that also covers the table, vibrating merrily against the green geometric carpet. The orange-lacquered dining chairs were covered in a fabric by Manuel Canovas, whom my father admired more than any other fabric designer.

ABOVE: The same chairs were used in the dining room, whose walls are painted in imitation of the Indian Rajput and Moghul treatment of dividing walls into panels using narrow bands of inlaid marble or cut plaster. The hard-edged abstract paintings, one on a graceful *Directoire* easel, are mixed with a Victorian statuette of Wellington and a ceramic relief of a native chief.

DAVID HICKS HOUSE,
ST LEONARD'S TERRACE, LONDON

My parents' London bedroom, decorated in the mid-
1960s with another of his torn-paper floral designs. The
vermilion carpet and shocking-pink felt curtains and
bedside tables suffuse the interior with a rosy glow that
somewhat mutes the effect of the pattern, whose stark
white ground is seen only on the roller blinds. The lamps
are of white glass. Like a Sleeping Beauty's chamber for
the 1960s, a tumbling, psychedelic, rose bower...

LORD & LADY JOHN CHOLMONDELEY, LONDON

BELOW & LEFT: My father created a penthouse suite of very modern rooms above the Cholmondeleys' more traditional apartment overlooking Hyde Park. The entrance to the new rooms has brilliant-orange distempered walls, stylishly outlined by an aubergine jute braid. As well as the Hicks 'Celtic' carpet, he also designed the bench and the base for the Van Struycken sculpture. The small study had curtains of brilliant-red suede against darkest-brown felt walls outlined by a narrow gold fillet.

RIGHT: The modern living room had an entire wall of glass, with the spectacular park view framed by white 'tweed' curtains edged in polished black leather. On the floor is a very large set of beige leather squab cushions. All the art and furniture was modern (unusually for a Hicks interior), including a wonderful early Hockney on the opposite wall.

MR & MRS MARK LITTMAN, LONDON

RIGHT: The Littmans' London drawing room was given stone-coloured walls and a chestnut parquet floor in 1966. The very simple white linen curtains were edged with narrow bands of shocking pink and scarlet, and similar colours covered the eighteenth-century chairs. The beige batik-covered drinks table and the snakeskin Parsons table blend perfectly with the walls. In the larger part of the room, single-ended sofas matched the curtains' white linen edged in pink and scarlet.

ABOVE: On a Genoese commode stands my father's portrait drawing of Marguerite Littman, with her trademark sunglasses, from the series that he made in 1966 and exhibited together with his sculptures.

MR & MRS MARK LITTMAN, LONDON

ABOVE: Marguerite Littman's dining room, the scene of many a famous lunch party, with its walls, window and table all dressed in a large-repeat flowered cotton. A single spotlight above the antler chandelier casts interesting shadows on the table. Daylight is filtered by white pinoleum blinds.

LEFT: In the master bedroom, the pinoleum blinds are green, as is everything except the off-white carpet and the white glass lamp. The green-and-white printed cotton is edged throughout in the same dark spinach-green wool as the lining of the bed. As my father said, the room 'looks like early summer' (*David Hicks on Living – with Taste*).

PRIVATE HOUSE, SUSSEX

LEFT: A circular sitting room in an oast house in Sussex was given a dramatic, nightclub feel in the late 1960s, tented with brilliant-red, scarlet, apple-green and purple stripes. On the apple-green carpet stand pink Perspex cube tables.

ABOVE: In the same seventeenth-century oast house, a beamed living room with an inglenook fireplace was brightened and updated with white paint, and metal and glass tables holding some early Turkish pottery. The rush matting on the floor and the rustic wood table are more traditional elements. They coordinate with the sofas – one in black-printed hessian, the other in a plain silver Thai cotton.

BELOW: Another rather untraditional English country room at the time, an old ballroom with a red ping-pong table and Joe Colombo chairs.

TWO ROOM-SETS, LONDON

LEFT: As one of the first professional interior designers in London, my father started doing room-sets in stores and exhibitions in the early 1960s. The small living room devised for Selfridge's in 1969 had highly lacquered red walls with narrow-banded paper borders dividing them into elegant panels. His 'Sammy' geometric carpet continued the red theme, complemented by the aubergine sofa with pink cushions (also his design) and magenta curtains.

BELOW: His earlier room for the Ideal Home Exhibition, 1967, was uncompromisingly modern, apart from the Louis XVI leather armchair behind the Perspex and glass desk. The cubic forms of the pink plastic armchair and stool echo his 'Palm Tree' sculpture (four dish mops), which appears in its orange Perspex case on the desk. The painting is by Mark Lancaster.

TWO LIVING ROOMS, LONDON

LEFT: A small London living room around 1968, the walls covered in Thai cotton, with a Bruce Tippett scroll-top painting hanging over one of a pair of striped sofas flanked by black lacquered Regency elbow chairs. The black painted wicker chair has a buttoned cushion in scarlet cotton, while the Hicks 'Y' carpet is red on a stone ground. The lighting is typically dramatic, by recessed ceiling downlights and artfully placed uplights.

ABOVE: Another living room, this one around 1971, with four satin-finish stainless-steel cube tables echoing the white, textured carpet's design of squares. A Joe Colombo chair faces an eighteenth-century cabinet and fauteuil, while the wall fabric continues as curtains.

THREE BEDROOMS, LONDON

ABOVE & RIGHT: Three interiors using my father's favourite device of outlining the form of the room or furniture with narrow bands of contrasting braid or paper. The mirrored dressing-table alcove (above left), around 1968, is outlined with paint; the blue 'tweed'-covered bedroom walls and bed (above right) are outlined with black braid, 1977; while the brown bedroom walls of 1970 (right) are outlined with a shiny red plastic border (matching the lampshades) on white braid, while bed, tables and curtains are all in beige silk with a dark-brown and white braid edging.

DAVID HICKS APARTMENT, PAULTON'S SQUARE, LONDON

LEFT & BELOW: 1974 saw us move from St Leonard's Terrace to this long, narrow, low-ceilinged apartment, which my father turned into an enfilade of small rooms painted cream throughout, united by the small-scale, mosaic-pattern carpet in cream, browns and black. Tall, narrow double doors opened on both sides of each room to give a sense of theatre, which was heightened by mirrors at the end that made endless reflections. One living room (left) had a white marble fireplace, lizard-skin tables and four swan-armed chairs; the other (below) had a sofa, bookcases and two tables for eating or writing, which could be pushed together if needed.

RIGHT: My bedroom (top right) had a castellated tester bed in a new Hicks fabric, continuing the beige theme; (below right) my sisters, instead, got pretty confections of pink and yellow glazed cotton trimmed with almond-green velvet ribbon, with one of the new Hicks wallpapers.

BELOW: The bedroom introduces green to the equation, with chairs in a pale-green 'tweed' that also edges the curtains of both bed and windows, which are in a pink Hicks 'Mint Flower' linen (also used to cover the table below the mirror). The long bench is covered in a dark olive shade of the same 'tweed'.

HYDE PARK HOTEL SUITE, LONDON

OPPOSITE & ABOVE:

Decorated in 1971, this suite of Edwardian panelled rooms was painted white throughout, ready for a quick injection of David Hicks colour. The living room is another of his vibrant games of reds and pinks, the thick bands of colour on cushions and curtains echoed in the abstract painting over the original marble chimneypiece. In *David Hicks on Decoration – 5*, he said that 'the gathered fabric lampshades are reminiscent of those in paintings by Vuillard'.

NIARCHOS APARTMENT,
GROSVENOR SQUARE, LONDON

LEFT & OPPOSITE: This nightclub-like interior was
created for the sons of Stavros Niarchos in 1972,
when they were in London studying. Not what
every student would think of as home, the
apartment was famously bizarre in daylight but
came alive by night. The walls are lacquered exactly
the brown of the suede banquette and the
textured Hicks carpet, on which his clear Perspex
cubes float surreally.

BELOW: Smoked-glass doors open on to the
stainless-steel-panelled dining room beyond, which
was nicknamed 'the kettle'. The steel panels float on
a red ground, with matching red curtains, cloth and
chairs linking back to the red sofa in the brown
living room.

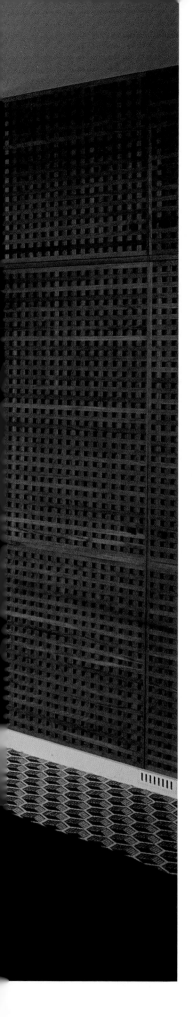

NIARCHOS APARTMENT,
GROSVENOR SQUARE, LONDON

LEFT: The master bedroom has Japanese-influenced wooden grilles over both wardrobes and windows (which have cunning red holland blinds to filter the harsh light of day). The walls are covered in grey flannel, also used quilted on the bed. The optical honeycomb carpet echoes the hexagonal motif on the spherical speakers.

RIGHT: Another Joe Colombo chair (top), with walls in black and white 'Clinch' and a loud Pop picture, provides the perfect telephone corner. The master bedroom's red-lacquer and aluminium desk (middle), beneath a tearful Roy Lichtenstein blonde, suggests intense study, and sets a theme continued in the second bedroom (bottom), with its 'Clinch' wallpaper in black on a silver foil ground, with beds and curtains in yet more red, and a silver Warhol of Marilyn Monroe.

TWO LIVING ROOMS, LONDON

OPPOSITE: In 1975, my father made a scheme for John Panchaud around a collection of abstract pictures. The DH Londonderry carpet of bold white, putty and brown octagons is taken up in the sofa covers and smoked-glass desk. The orange cushions pick out instead the orange picture reflected in the tall sheet of mirror – exactly the width of the fireplace – which is simply stuck to the wall.

ABOVE: A 1978 living room based around a collection of Chinese antiquities. Two mirrored alcoves hold vases of a single colour, the muted interior of pink and beige bringing out their vibrant yellow and maroon glazes. The textured carpet is in two tones of biscuit.

RIGHT: In the same 1930s Chelsea house, a Chinese Buddha head in the bay window is lit by a single spotlight. Eight suede floor cushions, stacked on the 'geo-floral' textured carpet, are ready to pull out as needed.

23 ST LEONARD'S TERRACE LONDON SW3 SLOANE 4652

I am giving a cocktail party with Waitman Martin
at 330 Decorative Center in Dallas from 6 to 8 on
Monday the 12th January and very much hope that
you will be able to come.

I much look forward to meeting you and showing
you my carpet designs and my new book 'David
Hicks on Living – with taste.'

Yours sincerely,

David Hicks.

Martin on enclosed card.

St. Leonard 16937/27

Hexagon 17088/4

Mr. Atle's Yacht 17037/27

Montpelier 17058/32

Celtic 17083/5

Wentworth 17111/10

Garden 17474/15

Buckingham Gate 17581/5

Daisy Tile 17584/2733

Persian Tile 17691/1

Diamond 17609/5

Period Flock 17077/15

Crown Jewels 17583/3

Pineapple 17582/12

Isle of Man 17663/6

Interlace 16954/4

Stained Glass Window 17690/1

Bubbles 17711/7

Basket Weave 17073/34

17427/1

Sam 17086/19

Rose Window 17653/1

Carpet Designs

Geometric Poppy 17097/4

Cross Crosslets 17134/22

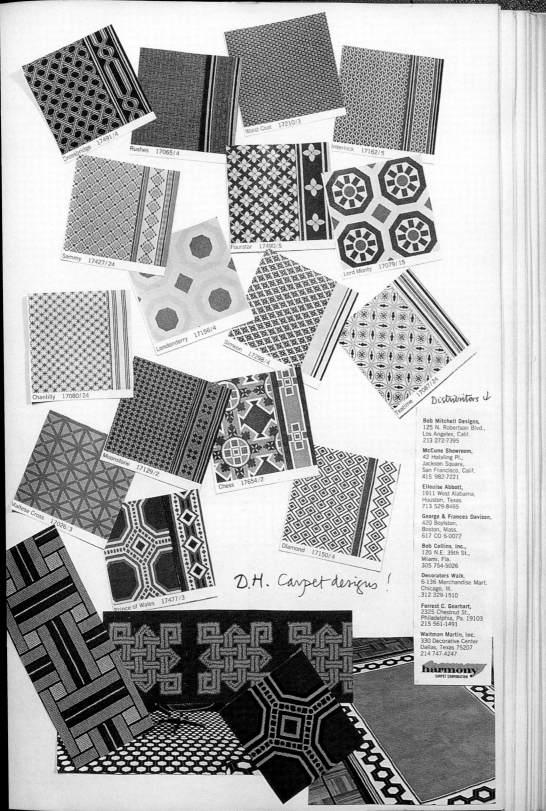

Waist-Coat 17210/3
Crossbridge 17491/4
Rushes 17065/4
Interlock 17162/5
Fourstar 17490/5
Lord Monty 17079/15
Sammy 17427/24
Londonderry 17156/4
Simeon 17298/4
Chantilly 17080/24
Teatime 17087/24
Moonstone 17129/2
Chess 17654/2
Maltese Cross 17026/3
Diamond 17150/4
Prince of Wales 17477/3

Distributors ↓

D.H. Carpet designs !

'David Hicks, London's most talked-about interior designer... David Hicks, the jet-propelled designer... After "David Hicks on living – with taste", Hicks should try a book entitled "David Hicks on Success",' proclaimed American magazines in 1967. With his ex-assistant-turned-associate, Mark Hampton, in New York to coordinate jobs; with fabrics, carpets, wallpaper and tiles of his design selling throughout the US; and with his books to promote the look, my father was ready to take on American designers on their home turf. The attractions of working in America soon paled – 'Now knockoffs of Hicks designs are seen walking along Third Avenue, not even Fifth. The dear Ladies who spread thousands of dollars wall-to-wall are not too happy' (*Home Furnishings Daily*, 1969) – but by then he had completed a number of very successful jobs. A small selection of these follow this page from his scrapbook for 1968.

MR & MRS MARK HAMPTON, NEW YORK

LEFT: When Mark and Duane Hampton married and moved back to New York, my father designed their first, tiny apartment as a wedding present. Unbeatably urbane and chic, it was entirely black and white, with stainless-steel screens and dramatic lighting. They soon moved into something larger (the apartment shown here), reusing the black, beige and white hexagon carpet, the Op Art-inspired fabric, and the white Perspex tables, gently introducing colour with beige walls and accents of red and yellow.

ABOVE: The Hamptons' bedroom, in contrast, is a riot of colour, with the handsome mouldings used as a sharp white frame for pink- and magenta-painted panels on the walls and two DH geometric fabrics in the same palette.

MR & MRS JOHN THEODORACOPOULOS, NEW YORK

ABOVE: This large Fifth Avenue apartment, decorated in 1969 for a Greek shipping magnate, had attractive pine panelling everywhere. My father painted this off-white, leaving the cornice, doors and architraves natural, creating a wooden frame for a white interior. The huge rug was woven to his design in Cogolin. He made new frames for the Foujita in white linen, and the Picasso over the fireplace, in stainless steel (which also lined the arched alcoves either side, filled with crystal objects).

RIGHT: Four unpainted Louis XV fauteuils combine with big sofas and Robsjohn-Gibbings 'Greek' leather stools by Saridis. Clear Perspex tables held cigarettes and ashtrays ('essentials' says *Decoration* – 5). Other Greek elements include antique vases under Hicks Perspex cases. Huge arrangements of dried flowers and grasses in galvanized iron buckets stand on Louis XV console tables in a masterpiece of understatement.

MR & MRS JOHN THEODORACOPOULOS, NEW YORK

ABOVE: The library (seen through the arch on the previous page) was left entirely in waxed, natural pine, except for the interiors of the bookcases, which were lacquered with white enamel. As a result, the white-cotton-covered hi-fi speaker and the air-conditioning grilles are almost invisible. A Louis XVI games table and fauteuils covered in yellow cotton sit happily between an armchair in Hicks 'Chevron' and a black leather banquette, while the small-repeat geometric rug signals a more intimate scale than the drawing room.

RIGHT: The dining room was dominated by a Japanese painted screen, which was mounted on slender stainless-steel uprights that allowed it to float eighteen inches above the floor. Massed dried flowers sit on a Boulle cabinet, while the dining table is made of glass with a bronze frame.

MR & MRS JOHN THEODORACOPOULOS,
NEW YORK

On the entrance-hall walls is stretched
rough hessian printed with my father's
favourite white impasto in his 'Clinch'
design (which also covers the sofa). The
hessian colour is continued in the wall-to-
wall coir matting. The pine architectural
frame delineates the space, as elsewhere.
A huge Dali Crucifixion is dramatically lit
with two white uplighters. The eighteenth-
century walnut table is crowded with
welcoming provisions.

MR & MRS JOHN THEODORACOPOULOS, NEW YORK

OPPOSITE: 'Betsy Theodoracopoulos and decorator David Hicks designed this beauty workshop together', enthused *Vogue*. 'Mirrors, mirrors on the walls, also on the ceiling. The wild mosaic of mirrors keeps its user well-informed on every angle of her, helps a dazzler get ready to dazzle in twenty minutes flat...' The hinged curtains of chrome beads, the rock-crystal objects on glass shelves, the professional hairdryer that lowers from the ceiling – all dazzling!

RIGHT & ABOVE: The bedroom was an all-white fantasy with yet more mirrors – in the shape of an elaborately engraved 1870 Sicilian looking glass over the fireplace, and bedside tables of mirror and chrome standing on the fur runners. The bed itself was coarse white 'tweed' on the outside, and glazed white cotton within.

MR & MRS FRANCIS FARR, LONG ISLAND

ABOVE: For Lydia Farr, my father made another all-white bedroom, this time using white-glazed Provençal floor tiles. The bed is hung outside with a large-scale damask design printed white impasto on white linen, with a shaped pelmet inspired by one he had seen at Drottningholm Palace in Sweden. The interior of the bed, again, is in glazed white cotton, and quilted. The stripped pine, antique wardrobe gives the only note of colour.

OPPOSITE: The Farr living room was dramatically modern: walls covered in small squares of cork, floor in rugged slabs of riven slate on which sat a shaggy brown tumble twist rug. 'Clinch' in white impasto on coarse brown linen makes Roman blinds at the window and a curtain framing the entrance. The abstract by John Rudge hangs over a chrome-framed blue marble fireplace. This is one of the very few Hicks rooms where everything is modern.

DAVID HICKS SUITE, ST REGIS HOTEL, NEW YORK

ABOVE: In 1970, my father was asked by this grand old hotel (built by Colonel Astor in 1904) to create a suite that would bear his name and be at his disposal whenever he was in the city. He loved the job, of course, especially having the handsome, panelled rooms and fine 1900 French furniture to play with. In the living room, seen here in daylight, he put simple, modern shelves with aluminium uprights for books, tables and sofas of his design, and some of Colonel Astor's chairs. The sofa and chairs are covered in plain Thai cottons, the colours picked from his own-design, torn-paper floral curtains.

OPPOSITE: The night view shows his dramatic lighting on the bleached white antelope heads – mounted on Perspex on the original marble chimneypiece – against the white-painted panelling. A mirrored screen in the corner and the mica table recall 1930s decorating by Syrie Maugham and Jean-Michel Frank.

DAVID HICKS SUITE,

ST REGIS HOTEL, NEW YORK

LEFT: Two colourways of a new geo-floral design, edged in lilac, were used to make the huge baldachin bed, which was (like all his curtained beds) simply screwed to the ceiling. The two armchairs are covered in solid colour picked from the bed fabric, and their frames have been freshly painted white.

OPPOSITE: The bathroom opened off the breakfast room, where a daybed of Hicks design was covered in brilliant grass green, echoing one of the prints above it. In the bathroom, with original marble floor and white tiles with a green border, 'H'-logo printed sheets were used to make shower curtain, basin valance, wall covering and lampshade, with the towels in the same colourway but in a slightly different scale.

ALAN VETERES APARTMENT, NEW YORK

LEFT: This typical modern apartment, with exposed concrete beams and parquet block floor, was given strong Hicks medicine in the form of wildly overscaled Arabic wallpaper in a strong colourway that covered both the walls and ceiling – not an easy sell to the average client! Rather than trying to hide the beams, my father accented them with bold terracotta paint, using burnt orange for the Roman blinds and Parsons table, on which sit two Hicks books. Chromed steel shelving, a fur blanket, Hicks 'Celtic' rug, and a mirror covered in small 'Hexagon' geometric complete the luxurious bachelor room.

ABOVE: The small bathroom gets a sense of excitement and space from walls and shower curtain in the same 'Hexagon' geometric. This works well with the checked tile floor.

Savannah is finished July 1969

SAVANAH
WINDEMERE ISLAND
ELEUTHERA
B W I

wrongly spelt paper by Tiffany

Romantic summers in a walled town

The David Hicks family
in the south of France

The playhouse, above, once a basket weaver's atelier, its big garden now turned into a swimming pool. Above, left: Next building but one to the clock tower, the Hickses' balconied summer haven—their main house. Left: Old top-floor granary in main house—a hideaway. If it has to, it can be a guest room, but more often it is an attic retreat for any one of the family who wants to climb the stairs to cat-nap, read a bit, or simply be alone. Above, right: In the main house library, on an antique commode, one of Mr. Hicks' still lifes: a porphyry urn filled with dried grasses from nearby fields, a little jar of potpourri, an arrangement of wood molds for cog-wheels.

alfway between Cannes and St. Tropez, the tiny medieval town of Roquebrune-sur-Argens hangs above the Mediterranean like a picturesque old eagle gone to roost. "Modernized" during the reign of Louis XVI, it is the picture-postcard kind of spot artists like to paint and —if they are incurable romantics like designer David Hicks—to live in. For six weeks of the summer and random weekends during the winter, he and his wife, Lady Pamela, fly from London to Nice with their three children, then drive along the seashore to their little town and their eighteenth-century summer house on the Rue de l'Horloge—so named because of the clock tower next door, the busiest building in town. It bongs off the hours like a French Big Ben, and on Sunday mornings sings a duet with the bells of the church behind the Hickses' house. "Really rather pleasant," says Mr. Hicks. "You can't sleep, of course, but no one minds."

The house is dated 1780, when it was rebuilt within a frame of ancient walls as indestructible as Carcassonne. It has always been a town house, however, and remains one. There is a little garden in the rear, but no outdoor space at all to soak up the sun in comfort. So the Hickses sought and found an annex, a much smaller structure, three minutes' walk away, that was once a basket weaver's atelier. Once the property was acquired, its sizable garden gave way to a swimming pool bordered by enough terrace space to lunch on.

The Hickses rise early, breakfast in their town house, then proceed in a family procession to the poolhouse to swim, tan, and do about lunch —the one meal at which they entertain. Mr. Hicks is the chef and a talented one (Lady Pamela never learned to cook and is happy now that she didn't). His specialty is a cold omelet stuffed, à la Niçoise, with black olives and a few other things you can guess at, but don't.

At dusk, the family goes "home," where the children have supper while their parents dress to go to dinner, alone or with guests, at one of the simple or grand restaurants that dot the Riviera like so many truffles.   (Continued)

←

Travel was always one of the great excitements and pleasures of my father's life and one of the richest influences on his work. He was a talented photographer – several of his books are illustrated almost entirely with his pictures – and his travel photographs from the early 60's, when he had the time to travel slowly with a good camera, are an interesting reflection of his creative vision. I have chosen a tiny selection of them to introduce two of his best houses, the ones that he made for our own holidays, in Roquebrune-sur-Argens in the south of France, and on the island of Eleuthera in the Bahamas. On this page, a spread from his scrapbook, with a feature on Roquebrune alongside the Bahamian house with its creator posing in full 1969 regalia, and his own-design writing paper for the house, annoyingly mis-spelt by Tiffany's.

INDIA

India, which my father first visited in 1962, was an enlightenment for him. The thrill of seeing the ultimate fantasy land first-hand, and in the greatest possible luxury (staying with the Prime Minister, the President and numerous Maharajahs just fifteen years after his father-in-law had been the last imperial Viceroy), was an overwhelming experience, especially since he and my mother saw everything almost alone, in the days before mass tourism was even imaginable.

RIGHT: The Taj Mahal from Shah Jahan's apartments in the fort at Agra. The old emperor was imprisoned here by his disloyal son Aurangzeb, forced to eke out his days in a cage that he himself had gilded.

THIS PAGE: Details of Fatehpur Sikri, Akbar's deserted capital: one of the mosque's gates, and a pierced marble Jali screen on the tomb of Sufi saint Shaikh Salim Chisti.

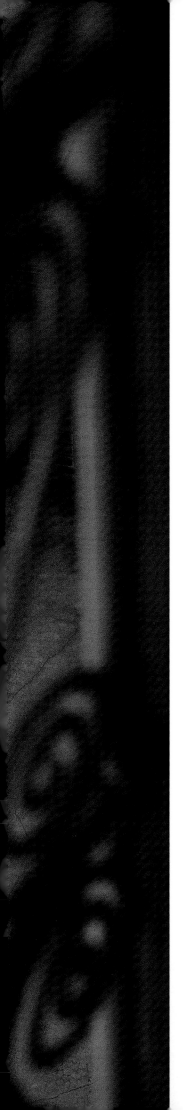

MOROCCO

My parents also visited Morocco in 1962, where my father again photographed every tiny detail, every clue of decorative inspiration that he saw. He loved the traditional Moucharabie screens, grilles of turned wood, and brought some back for his London studio windows. He photographed shops in the souk, sun loungers at the Hotel Mamounia, York Castle in Tangier.

LEFT: This picture of a courtyard, with a central fountain (an eight-pointed star), is seen through blurred metalwork.

ABOVE: A section of traditional Zelige mosaic work, whose elaborate Islamic geometry fascinated him, although he would never use anything so 'fussy' in his own work.

PERSIA

My parents went to Persia in 1965, while it was still Persia, and ever afterwards my father refused to call the country by any other name. They visited the Shah's palace in Teheran, where my father photographed extravagantly mirrored rooms and details like one of the telephones, in turquoise plastic with a huge, gold imperial crown. He photographed small objects in the museums and huge monuments alike, but it was Isfahan – the splendid capital established by Shah Abbas in 1590 – that bewitched him.

ABOVE & RIGHT: These two pictures show the earlier Ali Mosque in Isfahan, which was first built under the Seljuk Sultan Sanjar in the twelfth century and redecorated under the Safavid Shah Ismail at the start of the sixteenth. My father found its expanses of geometrically decorated bare brick, with the occasional accents of turquoise and blue tile, very exciting.

AFRICA

Travels in Africa ranged across the continent. One especially fat and luxurious album is filled only with my father's very large black-and-white pictures of the early, extraordinarily beautiful bronze and terracotta heads in the collection of the Oni of Ife in Nigeria. In the early 1960s, my parents visited Egypt, Sudan, all over West Africa, South Africa and Kenya.

FAR LEFT: In this picture of a religious procession in Axum, ancient capital of Ethiopia, a young Coptic priest holds aloft a glorious, almost Celtic-looking, gold cross. I love the blurred pink flowers against the geometric cross – very like an early Hicks room.

LEFT: In front of the rock-cut church at Axum, an older priest unwraps a cross of greater simplicity than the one on the opposite page.

ABOVE: This group of dancing children in Ghana wear fabrics that make even the strongest Hicks colourway look tame.

DAVID HICKS HOUSE, ROQUEBRUNE-SUR-ARGENS

OPPOSITE & LEFT: 8, Place de l'Horloge, Roquebrune-sur-Argens was a handsome eighteenth-century house on the main square in what was in 1966 (when my parents bought the house) an utterly unspoiled, sleepy southern French town. An almost entirely white living room, seen through the arched doorway from the oval staircase, had only two elements of colour: the original terracotta-tiled floor and a weathered, fifteenth-century Chinese wooden Buddha, bought in Japan, floating serenely on a glass table with skinny legs of steel. Beside the Buddha hung four Tahitian shell leis, and an abstract picture by Peter Sedgely. The table between the windows is a Hicks design, as is the Cogolin textured rug. The contrast of forms between the chairs – two by Kjaerholm, one Victorian, and the other a modern, fibreglass armchair – is accentuated by them all being white against the whitewashed walls. Unseen is a large white plastic-covered sofa.

RIGHT: The study had more colour, mainly found in the old Moroccan rug, from which my father picked out orange for the folding floor cushion and the steel base of the porphyry table, and scarlet for the sofa (all of which were designed by him). Above the sofa he hung a Denis Wirth-Miller landscape. The chandelier was white porcelain.

DAVID HICKS HOUSE, ROQUEBRUNE-SUR-ARGENS

LEFT & ABOVE: After a couple of years, my father bought a neighbouring property (a derelict workshop with a large yard). He made a swimming pool and garden, turning the workshop into a large pool pavilion. There he would give summer lunch parties, pushing together four small tables covered in his black-and-white 'Clinch' fabric, which were otherwise kept apart, in the corners of the room. Light cotton curtains, local raffia matting, cane blinds and bead curtains at the door continued the cool, airy theme of the whitewashed walls and beams. Two Edwardian Ionic columns from London, stripped of their paint, flanked the stylized beach scene.

DAVID HICKS HOUSE, ROQUEBRUNE-SUR-ARGENS

OPPOSITE: The master bedroom began life in a Spartan, contemplative spirit, with the bed standing without curtains in the centre of the room and a 1937 Empire-style swan chair at each corner. It was not long before my father felt the urge to drape it 'to give it warmth'. He used his 'Zed' print in pale pink and orange, with orange edging and blankets, which worked with the tile floor and original 1810 chimneypiece (on which he placed an especially fine Empire ormolu incense burner). The chairs' velvet covers match the terracotta floor, while shaggy goatskin rugs added a further note of luxury.

ABOVE: He cut the bathroom by placing the bath to one side of the chimney, like Jefferson's bed at Monticello, thus creating a separate dressing room beyond. A corresponding door to the left opened on to a tiny loo. Again, everything is white, apart from the black-and-white Moroccan rug and the slight tones of pale-pink towels and faded blue Perspex case for one of his sculptures, this one an old hinge.

DAVID HICKS HOUSE, ROQUEBRUNE-SUR-ARGENS

ABOVE LEFT: In my bedroom, the bed is hung with the same 'H'-logo design in which I slept in England (also used to cover this book). The rug is Indian, and the bedside table is an English country one belonging to Iris Hicks.

ABOVE RIGHT: An attic guest room with an old half-baldachin, which my father found in the room and reused with simple white cotton hangings.

BELOW: My sisters' room, which contains another colourway of the 'H'-logo design on beds and lampshades alike. My father's painting of Britwell Hill, which could be seen from our house in the country, sits over the fireplace.

OPPOSITE: This guest room opened off the hall on the ground floor. My father found the rustic beams above a collapsing plaster ceiling. He decided to make a feature of these beams, placing a smooth aluminium downlighter on the rough surface. The daybed in ochre leather has a fur rug as a bedspread, while the Provençal armoire is lined with turquoise cotton.

SAVANNAH, ELEUTHERA, BAHAMAS

BELOW: My father built this house for us in 1969, with Nassau architect Robert Stokes. Inspired by the temple/tomb complex of King Zoser at Saqqara of 2680 BC, which he had seen five years before, the house was a little unexpected in its setting, since every other house on the island tried to ape the local Colonial style of pretty pastel colours and clapboard. These exterior pictures of the newly finished house, surrounded by sand on which grass has not yet begun to grow, bring my father's Egyptian fantasy perfectly to life.

LEFT: The house is entered through a roofed, screened-in porch, off which all the rooms open. Here it is seen as it was when first finished, before the midday heat prompted my father to make the whole roof solid. In this cool porch we ate, studied and played cards at a large Formica table, made by a local carpenter to a Hicks design when the one shown here proved too small.

LEFT: The monumental entryway so dramatically photographed here is somewhat smaller than it looks. Two towering, freestanding pylons flank the entrance. These serve no practical purpose besides looking splendid and casting interesting shadows as the sun goes down between them, reflected in the distant water of Savannah Sound.

SAVANNAH, ELEUTHERA, BAHAMAS

ABOVE & RIGHT: The living room at Savannah was cool, fresh and airy, dominated by the two large scroll-top pictures specially painted by Bruce Tippett (the Caribbean colours doubtless specified by Hicks). The floors and walls throughout the house were roughly plastered with a mixture of local pink sand from the Atlantic beach in front, plus cement and marble dust, raked with nails on a board to give an interesting texture. The ceilings, by contrast, were of smooth white plaster, floating with a narrow, black-painted gap all around. Every window and door reached up to the ceiling, to emphasize the house's monumental stature. White and yellow Perspex cube tables, buttoned sofas and sculptures are all by my father, while the white pottery stag was made by my cousin, Michael-John Knatchbull. A huge rug of coir matting sits on the floor. The windows, which slid back into the walls on the rare occasions when the air conditioning was not chilling the air, have opaque white roller blinds.

Ten

1971
1972

Britwell Books Limited

IN WHITE HOUSE ALLEY

43 Conduit Street
London W1R 0NL
Telephone: 01 437 7722
Telex: 21820
Cables: Gubuhic London W1

Invoice

New York Times Sep 18 1971 DH wallpaper

United Press International

Mr. Nixon, unfazed by photographers and newsmen, then rolled a strike on second lane. He said his average was 152.

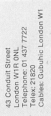

DH writing paper design

David Hicks Limited

vogue 71

David Hicks has put his patterns on
American sheets and towels, *right*. His letter
H on non-iron sheets, geometric cables on
towels. Blues, suede browns, more colours,
patterns, at Heal's; Tiarco, 47 Beauchamp Pl.

Some years ago in London
I worked with Adelle Donen,
who married the man who
made the film Seven Brides
For Seven Brothers, Cha-
rade and many other star-
studded films. It was in
Stanley Donen's flamboyant
London apartment that I
first met David Hicks who
had done its interior design.

It has been a few years
now, but our paths crossed
again on Thursday night.
He had just flown in from
London to confer with the
NSW Government, for which
he is designing our new
London offices under the
aegis of Sir Jock Pagan. We
met at Happy and Dolly
Robertson Ward's super
Christmas party. A tre-
mendous assembly of well
known faces were gathered
to enjoy their marvellous
hospitality.

Sydney paper

The David Hicks Suite / St Regis Hotel, New York City

From David Hicks

David Hicks Limited

23 St Leonards Terrace
London SW3
Telephone 01-730 4652
Telex: 21820
Cables: Gubuhic London W1

DAVID HICKS

Ha pasado por Madrid como un relámpago. Viene a decorar una casa en Puerta de Hierro. A primera hora de la mañana tiene una reunión en Casa y Jardín, empresa con la que piensa trabajar en el futuro. En el bolsillo, un billete de avión para volver a Londres a mediodía. A pesar de su horario apretado, David Hicks encuentra una hora para compartir sus ideas sobre esa técnica y ese arte, nada fácil, de la decoración de interiores. Y lo hace con calma, como si en un tiempo indefinido no tuviese otra cosa que hacer, sino contestar a todas mis preguntas. Gran resorte psicológico y temperamental de los ingleses, que saben compaginar la máxima tensión interior con la calma más aplastante.

Habla despacio, escucha con interés, sonríe plácidamente, posa sin pestañear cuantas veces se le pida. En tres meses ha dado la vuelta al mundo, no por una apuesta a lo Philleas Fogg, sino para resolver una serie de proyectos de mucha envergadura y no menos millones de libras. Pesan sobre sus hombros trabajos encargados por el Gobierno de Australia y de Londres, por particulares de Miami o de Suiza, por empresas textiles o por los tradicionales propietarios del Club de Hombres de la Ciudad de Londres. Encargos que le preocupan, aunque por su modo de hablar se adivina que disfruta tanto con cada uno, que más parece que se trata de un «hobby» que de una gran responsabilidad. Me asegura, sin embargo, y se lo acepto, que el trabajo es duro. Exige una dedicación completa, física e incluso espiritual, tan total que ni en los mejores momentos de sus vacaciones puede olvidarse de lo que lleva entre manos. Y es natural.

QUE TRABAJA PARA LOS CINCO CONTINENTES

Para un artista, cualquier pequeño aliento de vida, el detalle más insignificante, puede resultar revelador.

—Háblenos del gran secreto de su decoración. Usted es un maestro en todo lo que suponga mezcla audaz de elementos, líneas, diseños y colores. ¿Cómo, cuándo y por qué hizo posible lo que parecía imposible?

—Las primeras ideas sobre decoración las tuve cuando era muy joven. Desde pequeño fui un rebelde, y esa postura vital me influyó de modo decisivo para mi carrera. El gusto de mi padre y de mi madre me aburrían. Y encontraba igual de aburridos los cuartos de los hoteles, las casas de nuestros amigos, todo lo que iba viendo a mi alrededor. Lo encontraba formal, conservador, triste.

—¿Cuántos años tenía cuando empezó a trabajar?

SIGUE

The 1970s saw the focus of my father's work shift from America to Europe, opening shops with associate designers in France, Switzerland, Belgium, Germany and Norway within a few years. This page from his 1972 scrapbook may have his St Regis writing paper and no fewer than three pictures of Nixon in his Hicks-papered White House bowling alley, but it is dominated by an article in Spanish *Telva* magazine on the designer 'who works on five continents'. Retreating from the New World sent him into Europe, where he continued to spread his message of pattern and colour with the same assurance and conviction as ever, perhaps now tempered with a little more experience. On the following pages are some of the best moments of Hicks in the 1970s – and just one in the 1980s.

COMTESSE DE FLEURS, PARIS

ABOVE: This apartment's immense double-height living room, reached from a high stair, needed to be made less cold and vertigo-inducing. He devised a huge pattern inspired by seventeenth-century damasks, which he printed in white impasto on a buff linen. The design's size shrunk the space, linking it to the small sitting room from which the stair descended. Huge ivory silk curtains are edged in the same scarlet as the sofa.

RIGHT: The awkward-shaped hall (too many doors) was simplified and given instant elegance, with painted panels and a dark border to the plain carpet outlining the space.

OPPOSITE: The dining room used a Cogolin carpet in scarlet and black on beige, and teamed with eighteenth-century wallpaper panels framed by brown marbleized paper. Curtains and screen in different 'Indienne' prints share the palette of the walls and rug.

PRIVATE HOUSE, SWITZERLAND

This living room in a house outside Geneva was decorated by my father in 1971 entirely in shades of white, except for the two armchairs covered in his 'Spanish Moss' green cotton. The only other colour is the narrow red line in the white braid that edges the off-white linen walls and curtains. The armless sofa, in the same linen, has cushions in Hicks geometrics, which provide the only pattern. The modern tables in stainless steel and glass (right) were designed by my father for the room. His chrome and smoked-glass cube (above) is a witty counterpoint to the simple, antique wood tables holding modern sculpture.

PRIVATE HOUSE, SWITZERLAND

OPPOSITE: In this pine library in Switzerland in 1970, my father kept the pine bookcases and doors natural, matching its colour with a caramel suede that he stretched in padded squares on the walls. The square motif recurs in the Cogolin textured carpet – in caramel on a bronze ground similar to the painting – and the same suede was used to cover the sofa.

PRIVATE HOUSES, SWITZERLAND

ABOVE: A small dining room in another Swiss house in 1974 again has bronze-painted walls, with modern interpretations of Regency klismos chairs around a circular table with one of the David Hicks 'Tarascon' printed cottons. The textured carpet in white is also a Hicks design.

RIGHT: This dining room, seen from the white living room shown on the previous page, makes a dramatic contrast to it but uses the same white linen for curtains (although here they are kept utterly simple, hanging from poles). White-beamed ceiling, doors and chimneybreast frame bronze-painted walls and a Hicks 'Celtic' fitted carpet in scarlet on bronze.

MR & MRS JOHN THEODORACOPOULOS, ATHENS

In 1971, my father decorated this penthouse apartment in Athens for the same Greek client (known as J. T.) for whom he had made one of his best interiors in New York. High up in an ugly modern building, it boasted a magnificent view of the Acropolis, seen at night (above) with two pieces of ancient sculpture and the owner's portrait by Dali dramatically lit by my father's trademark uplighters, enamelled white to suit the mainly white interior. (Left) The view from the glass-topped, beige leather desk at one end of the living room shows how my father solved the problem of badly proportioned, low windows – plates of mirror above them and full-length curtains of scarlet Thai silk. White-'tweed'-covered walls are divided into panels by satin-finish stainless steel, while bronzes of Greek athletes compete in a miniature Olympiad on Hicks-designed marble and Perspex bases.

MR & MRS JOHN THEODORACOPOULOS,
ATHENS

RIGHT: This view looks back towards the
beige leather and chrome desk, which is
screened by a curtain of chrome beads
from the dining area beyond. The
righthand wall is entirely mirrored, with
mirrored niches for glass shelves, on
which ancient pottery and books are
arranged, and the full-length red curtains
making strong verticals. The other wall is
all steel-framed panels of white 'tweed'.
On each of these panels there hangs an
old master, framed with a narrow band
of stainless steel and lit by chrome
picture lights. Two huge, textured white
Cogolin rugs sit on the floor, of white
marble. The four Louis XVI fauteuils are
all upholstered in cut velvet.

MR & MRS JOHN THEODORACOPOULOS, ATHENS

ABOVE: The entrance hall of the apartment, whose naive 1970s interpretation of ancient architecture was already in place when my father arrived on the scene, was furnished with modern chairs in black lacquer and a thick glass table supported by antique marble lions.

OPPOSITE: The dining area lay between the hall and J. T.'s desk, screened by the curtain of chrome beads. The doors and overdoors were covered in the same beige leather as the desk. Between them, my father hung the big Dali Crucifixion from the New York entrance hall. Lit by a single white downlighter, the glass dining table and black lacquered chairs stood on the second white Cogolin rug, which continued past the bead curtain and underneath the desk.

BARONSCOURT, NORTHERN IRELAND

ABOVE & OPPOSITE: This great house, built in the 1780s by Steuart and then Soane (and remodelled internally by William Vitruvius Morrison in the 1830s) was decorated by my father in the mid-1970s. He loved the job more than almost any other, for the clients, now Duke and Duchess of Abercorn, were great friends, with wonderful possessions for him to arrange in vast rooms with splendid, rich late Greek revival plasterwork. Together, they brought the house back to life, making it modern and clean. The Long Gallery had been divided into three rooms in the 1930s. My father delighted in taking down the clumsy partitions and restoring the space to its original glory. He painted the plasterwork white, with panelled walls in two shades of stone, and used a giant damask-printed white-on-natural linen at the windows, retaining the Victorian curtain poles' aged gilding along with the oil chandeliers. Simple, modern sofas and fine antique furniture found in the attics and cellars were covered with plain fabrics – some more muted than others.

BARONSCOURT, NORTHERN IRELAND

LEFT: The hall was painted in two tones of warm apricot pink, framed in white. Three marble busts, three carved Abercorn crests (a tree being sawn) and a huge rug complete the picture.

BELOW: The central Rotunda, looking through to the Long Gallery, was brightened with buttercup-yellow paint, its frieze picked out in pale lettuce green. A glazed cotton cloth of the same green is always kept on the large circular table. When the room is used as a dining room, a linen tablecloth is placed on top.

OPPOSITE: A Family Room was created in the enormous old ballroom. Ceiling spotlights make an exciting backdrop for this practical room with dining, sitting and kitchen areas, divided by green-stained wood and white Formica kitchen units.

LEFT: The monumental staircase hall was given strong Hicks treatment: deep-scarlet walls, with the fine Neoclassical architecture painted white, framing a series of family portraits, which are lit by picture lights. Otherwise, it is sparsely furnished, as halls should be.

BELOW: The library, which opens off the staircase hall, is a feast of pattern and colour, however. The scarlet of the hall is continued here as the ground of the bold carpet, and again it picks out the plasterwork frieze and the interior of the wood-grained bookcases, making the old leather bindings glow like gold. Two large DH sofas are covered in his geometrics, while the old dining-room curtains of claret velvet were stretched above the bookcases and around the fireplace. This is a wonderfully warm room, boldly modern but still full of history.

VILA VERDE, ALGARVE, PORTUGAL

OPPOSITE: In 1982, my father chose the site and designed the architecture, interiors and garden for the Ghanis' new house, which he considered to be the great, definitive project of his life. Lit dramatically at night is one of the three towering porticoes (here seen across the swimming pool), modelled very closely on Inigo Jones' 'Tuscan Barn' church of St Paul's, in Covent Garden, but executed entirely in concrete. The house walls are plastered with a rough cement finish concocted on site using terracotta colouring, gravel and seashells, in contrast with the smooth, painted cement details.

ABOVE: The staircase hall has a floor of polished stone. This reflects the Hicks-designed rusticated water feature, which drips constantly, and is wonderfully cooling on a hot day. The hall is lined with grey paper, while the staircase and balusters, again, are formed from concrete.

VILA VERDE, ALGARVE, PORTUGAL

ABOVE: My father's own room in the Ghanis' house opens off the staircase hall and the loggia by the pool. He insisted on having only his own possessions in here, from a Poterie d'Apt chimneypiece from Roquebrune to the collages by the bed that he made with old pictures of his childhood, including his long-lost older brother, John. The floor is of polished, stained terrazzo, inspired by one in Venice; the bath, at the foot of the bed, is encased in granite.

OPPOSITE: The Great Room at Vila Verde, an immense, double-height space in the centre of the house. On the walls is raw artists' canvas; on the floor is a carpet inspired by a seventeenth-century Persian document, designed (like all the furniture) for the room. The chimneypiece in Violette de Breche marble and the bust of King George III are carefully matched to the room's huge scale. Through the doors is the dining room; above is a more intimate living room.

Japan

This last section focuses on my father's own last houses, and his last shop, which opened in 1978. He personally did less and less interior design as time passed, giving his name to mediocre, commercial jobs carried out by assistants, while he focused his own much greater talent and still-thriving creativity on other things: gardens, jewellery or the perfection of his funeral arrangements. He lived in his Oxfordshire garden, coaxing and teasing it into an extraordinary sequence of green rooms that never failed to satisfy him, as each year he waited with mounting excitement for the new tulips or peonies, bought from a catalogue in deepest winter, to burst forth. He still loved to travel, but disliked much of what he saw in the modern world. He was happiest at home in the country, where he laboured on his flowers, his garden and his scrapbooks: here, a page of Japan, laid out with his usual panache.

DAVID HICKS SET, ALBANY, PICCADILLY, LONDON

RIGHT: My father was working on this set (of rooms) when *Living with Design* was published in 1979. The narrow entrance hall was entirely covered in marbleised paper, with that favourite Hicks device of a jib or concealed door with a small, lit vitrine table that moved with the door.

OPPOSITE & BELOW: Living room and bedroom are treated as one, painted in a matt Venetian red, with his 'Indian'-design carpet in orange, maroon and bronze. Vermilion cotton covered my grandmother's swan chairs; magenta wool, the Louis XV fauteuils. Oval portraits hung from scarlet silk damask ribbons (remains of the Britwell dining-room curtains, the bulk of which dress the splendid bed's interior).

DAVID HICKS SHOP, JERMYN STREET, LONDON

My father opened his last shop in 1978, just across Piccadilly from his set at Albany. Unlike earlier David Hicks shops, this was very large, more showroom than shop, with a sequence of elaborate, formal room-settings that were changed every few months. (Above) The front was nothing if not imposing, with the slick bronze columns and 'H'-logo door handle. (Opposite & below) Within, a riot of colour burst forth: quilted, orange glazed cotton cloths on triangular tables; abstracted desert sunsets by Rib Bloomfield; dhurries in Hicks designs; and quantities of accessories – plastic, ceramic, antique or modern.

DAVID HICKS SHOP, JERMYN STREET, LONDON

LEFT: The intimidating approach to my father's office at the back of the new shop, with his minimalist white Formica desk and scarlet 'tweed' chairs.

OPPOSITE & BELOW: Two more room-settings in the shop, which were divided by an enormous 'H' logo on the floor, in dark wood and doormat, the edge of which can be seen to the right of the bed. Curtains of maroon tweed adorn the bed, using shiny glazed cotton in pink for the lining, and scarlet for the edging. The sitting room has a similar mixture, with a Denis Wirth-Miller landscape hung between architectural engravings.

DAVID HICKS SET,
ALBANY, PICCADILLY, LONDON

After fifteen years, my father tired of his red
magnificence and wanted something
cleaner, fresher, a little more modern.

LEFT & RIGHT: Walls of Vandyke brown, the
old eagle tables given new fossil-stone tops,
a curious floor in pale beige linoleum –
these were the ingredients of the new set.
Saying that Albany was not a place for
women, he banished the female portraits,
keeping only my mother's male ancestors.
The bulging red festoon blinds of before
were replaced by vertical slatted louvres of
birch, copied from some in Sir John Soane's
dressing room.

ABOVE: His new bed was smaller, but still
imposing, with the swan chairs lined up
before it and a cast of an ancient relief set
into the wall above.

THE GROVE

LEFT: In 1990 my father designed this pavilion in the middle of the elaborate garden that he had spent the previous ten years creating. The pavilion was my mother's sixtieth birthday present to him: she had learned many years before that the only presents he enjoyed were ones that he has designed, or at least chosen, himself. The lower room is reached by means of a small drawbridge; the upper one, by an outside stair.

ABOVE: The Secret Garden beside the pavilion – seen here in full, overpowering bloom on an early June morning – is enclosed by the old-brick garden walls of the simple farmhouse The Grove used to be. A heady mixture inside of old and new roses, peonies, huge papery poppies and an abundance of cheeky, swaying foxgloves creates a confusion of colour and scent for a few weeks every summer that was my father's great joy.

THE GROVE

OPPOSITE: The hornbeam stilt trees, with hornbeam hedges behind them, were planted in 1979, and my father waited impatiently for them to thicken enough to make his vision of green architecture a reality. This part of the garden is composed, like a proscenium stage, around the view from the drawing-room window. The stone urns came from Britwell.

ABOVE: The hall has a floor of waxed York stone flags, its walls papered in a golden colour, with a wide brown band defining their edges. Over the library door is my grandfather's crest, removed from Viceregal Lodge, Simla when he left India. Bookshelves can be seen through the door, as can the red and blue 'Turkey carpet'. His gardening boots are ever ready beneath the hall table.

THE GROVE

OPPOSITE: The drawing room at The Grove was added to the house in 1790 and is the only large room. My father hung it with pink cotton, creating some very pretty, feminine curtains, swagged with ruched borders, for the big window. He also made a chimneypiece in natural wood with inlaid panels of Formica banding – the only modern element in the room (though he replaced it ten years later with an antique white marble one). The big Regency mirror on the chimneybreast came from his library at Britwell.

ABOVE: When we moved to The Grove from Britwell, the Rex Whistler panels from my mother's study came too, of course, becoming the dining room of this much smaller house. My father took Edwardian mahogany dining chairs and painted them off-white, covering them with a turquoise cloth that went well with the walls.

THE GROVE

ABOVE: My father's bedroom ('one likes one's own room in the autumn of one's life') has a bath in an alcove, the loo in a cupboard beside it, and an uncomfortably low washbasin set into a bookcase – low, so not to obstruct the view of his growing garden from the bed, which came from the Oak Room at Britwell.

LEFT: Either side of the bed are his memorabilia cabinets, already well stuffed. Shortly before he died, my father rearranged these entirely, and the room too, moving the bed to face the bath. This gave him a better view of his now-full-grown hornbeam stilt trees.

Index

Page numbers in italics refer to captions

David and Pamela Hicks in their London living room, 1970

Acknowlegdements

The author and publishers would like to thank John Spragg, without whose help The Estate of David Hicks photographic archive, on which this book is based, would not have survived. The author and publishers would like to acknowledge the work of the following photographers included within this book: © Jacques Bachmann, © Pierre Berdoy, © Michael Boys, © Roger Guillemot, © Jon Harris, © Pascal Hinous, © Nicholas Jenkins, © Michel Lavrillier, © Patrick Lichfield, © Norman McGrath, © Derry Moore, © James Mortimer, © Michel Nahmias, © Hans Namuth, © John Spragg, © Edward Woodman.

ADDITIONAL PHOTOGRAPHY:

Vila Verde on pp192-195 © Mark Fiennes/Country Life Picture Library.
Savannah, Eleuthera on pp.168–171 © 1991 Hans Namuth Estate Courtesy, Center for Creative Photography, The University of Arizona.

The publishers have attempted to contact the copyright owners of the images published in this book. The publisher apologises if inadvertently permission has not been obtained.

LO